D0453987

Vegan Delights

VEGAN DELIGHTS

Jeanne Marie Martin

HARBOUR PUBLISHING

Published by:
HARBOUR PUBLISHING
P.O. Box 219
Madeira Park, BC Canada V0N 2H0

Cover design and illustration by Kelly Brooks
Printed and bound in Canada

Canadian Cataloguing in Publication Data

Martin, Jeanne Marie, 1951–
    Vegan delights

    Includes index.
    ISBN 1-55017-079-1

    1. Vegetarian cookery.   I. Title.
TX837.M37 1993   641.5'636   C93-091354-X

To my dear friend
Greg G. Semkuley
You have been like a brother to me.
Thank you for your love and
support and for believing in me.
Many of these recipes were created
in your kitchen.

ACKNOWLEDGEMENTS

Special thanks and appreciation to my dear friends Kitty Cates, Samaya Ryane, June and Loring Windblad, Maria Matsen and Andrew Piers for their inspiration, enthusiasm and love.

My heartfelt appreciation to my terrific editor Mary Schendlinger for her expert help.

Also thanks to Valeria Deyong, Healer, Rose Marie Woloch, R.M.T. and Dr. Roger H. Rogers, M.D. for their healing hands and hearts.

And my gratitude to God for the creative energy, healing and strength to complete this work.

Contents

Foreword

Dr. David Wang, B.Sc., N.D.
Burrard Integrated Health Clinic
Vancouver, British Columbia

As a Naturopathic Physician, I have always emphasized the role of sound nutrition as a major part of the healing process. For people moving toward vegetarianism, good nutrition has to be more than salads and tofu, it has to look, smell and taste delectable. *Vegan Delights* is a welcome sight to my patients as they embark on a natural path to optimal health—no kitchen should be without such an insightful and tempting cookbook.

Modern health problems which have emerged or multiplied over the last few decades, especially in industrialized nations, have physicians baffled. Many of these diseases can be attributed to lifestyle factors, especially problems of overconsumption—high cholesterol, fat, mucus-forming foods, and exogenous toxins (namely meats and dairies)—and the lack of fibre and high-water content foods (namely vegetables).

In light of cross-cultural studies, and evidence that a meat- and dairy-centred diet has been implicated in many major diseases, one should at least consider shifting to a vegetable-rich diet. This preventive lifestyle choice will benefit many who adopt it, by substantially lowering the risk of heart disease, diabetes, hypertension, breast and colon cancers, and generally improving their well-being.

For these reasons, I recommend *Vegan Delights* to all physicians and patients alike. Whether or not you are a "pure" vegan, the tasty recipes in this book are proof that healthier foods can be delicious too. One of Jeanne Marie's greatest attributes is her skill to create gourmet vegetarian recipes. Like her previous books, *The All Natural Allergy Cookbook* and *Hearty Vegetarian Soups and Stews*, this collection of creative recipes and helpful cooking and nutrition tips will be received by my patients with much delight.

Jeanne Marie Martin is one of the foremost authorities in creating nutritious and delicious dishes. Her passion to share her knowledge grew out of her personal triumph over allergies, chronic fatigue syndrome and Candida. In this authoritative new book, Jeanne Marie shares her expertise and gives us the benefit of her twenty-two years' experience in the field of nutrition and health. The wealth of information in her work provides the elements needed to forge a lifestyle that can lead to health and longevity. Practical, succinct chapters on the details of what to look for in choosing and preparing foods take us from theory to practical application; we emerge with both understanding and a useful everyday guide to healthy eating. Enjoy!

About the Author

Jeanne Marie Martin lectures internationally on topics concerning natural foods and wholistic lifestyles. Her twenty-two years' experience has led her to write five health cookbooks and over 150 magazine articles. She specializes in creating special diets for people with allergies, Candida Albicans, chronic fatigue syndrome, high or low blood sugar, heart problems and weight control problems. Jeanne Marie offers nutritional consultations through the Burrard Integrated Health Clinic in Vancouver and is the primary cooking instructor for the Alive Academy of Nutrition in Burnaby, BC.

Ms. Martin is also the food editor for *Total Health*, an international magazine based in California. Several North American periodicals publish her articles and columns regularly, including *Alive* health magazine of Canada; *Shared Vision*, a new age magazine; *Fittingly Yours* and *Vancouver Health and Fitness*, sports and fitness magazines.

Ms. Martin is a frequent speaker for universities, hospitals, clinics, TV and radio. For lecture information or nutritional consultations in writing or by telephone, write: P.O. Box 4391, Vancouver, BC Canada V6B 3Z8.

The Vegan Diet: Do It Right

This book was born for two reasons: 1) I feel that the Vegan Diet is a beautiful and wholesome diet which is beneficial to the planet's healthy environment when properly followed; and 2) I am concerned about the numbers of people I meet and talk to in my cooking classes and private nutritional consultations, who are attempting to follow a vegan diet but are unaware of basic nutrient needs and meal planning options that are essential for optimum health and full enjoyment of the diet.

The Vegan Diet is a vegetarian diet that excludes all forms of animal products: meat, poultry, fish, seafood, eggs, dairy products, gelatin and honey, along with any products that are processed with these ingredients, like refined white sugar. All food products that come from living creatures, even bees, are eliminated.

The Vegan Diet is growing in popularity, especially due to the work of John Robbins and Dr. Michael Klaper, M.D. The Vegan Diet is not a new idea. I was aware of it over fifteen years ago when I wrote my first cookbook, *For the Love of Food*, and it was included in the diet plans of that book. Back then, vegan was pronounced VEG-an, with a soft "g" as in vegetable. Now it is more commonly pronounced VEE-gan or VAY-gan, with a hard "g" as in garden.

The main motivations for this diet are: 1) health, 2) the environment and 3) spirituality.

With the rising incidence of health problems, especially allergies, heart disease, cancer and arthritis, more and more people are choosing to eliminate or at least reduce animal foods in the diet, as there is evidence that they aggravate most diseases.

As so aptly pointed out by Frances Moore Lappé in *Diet for a Small Planet* and John Robbins in *Diet for a New America*, it takes far less energy, water, food, land and money to raise vegetable foods than it does to raise animals for meat and dairy products. The Vegan Diet also helps protect the fragile eco-balance of our environment.

Some people believe it is morally and spiritually wrong to kill or abuse animals in any way for the purpose of "pleasure" foods for humans. Most of us could not bring ourselves to kill an animal for food, yet we allow ourselves to eat what another has killed.

It has been well proven that humans can not only exist but can thrive on a well-balanced diet without animal products, and it helps our environment as well. The authors mentioned above and others listed in the Books section (page 216) have gathered information that supports these facts. Taking all of this into consideration, you might conclude that it is wise to be on a Vegan Diet or at least cut back on animal product consumption.

It is important to support people wherever they are with their diet and encourage them to make changes on their own, in their own time. Many are led to vegetarian diets and veganism by taking simple steps away from animal products toward alternatives that are easy, nonthreatening and accessible. Providing attractive foods in widely varied recipes and menu ideas that satisfy the taste buds, while generously supplying needed vitamins and minerals, does more to promote this diet than insisting people change completely.

An important aspect of this and all diets is to ensure not only good, nutritious foods for vegans but to make sure the foods are properly prepared to assist proper digestion and assimilation. I believe we are not "what we eat" so much as what we absorb!

In my private diet consultations and classroom lectures, vegans have made repeated complaints, including some of the following: "I get so cold all the time. I don't seem to have enough body heat, even in summer." This need never be a problem for vegans. Unfortunately, many vegans choose to consume mainly raw foods. While a raw diet may work well in California, Hawaii, Texas, Florida, Mexico, other tropical countries or in summertime elsewhere, it is far from appropriate or healthful to the average person living in cooler climates. I say *average* because some healthy individuals can eat raw foods and survive well in almost any climate. But this is the exception, not the rule. Most people require some cooked foods as fuel, and those who have trouble "keeping warm" will find that warm cooked whole grains (5–12 servings per week) and *tender*, cooked legumes (beans, peas and lentils): 3–10 servings per week) will help them reach and maintain normal body temperatures. People who have trouble digesting these foods should enlist the proper cooking techniques mentioned in this book and use digestive aids if necessary to assist the body until the digestive system can adapt.

Another common complaint from vegans is the lack of variety in the diet. A perusal of this book's recipes and menus will offer *abundant* relief from the doldrums of a "rabbit food" and "bird seed" diet.

Some vegans have brittle hair and nails and poor skin tone. These conditions can be greatly helped by a balanced diet that includes whole grains and legumes, nuts and seeds, dark leafy green vegetables, green herbs, seaweeds, nutritional yeast, barley green, flax seeds and oil and protein foods. Other helpful supplements include horsetail/silica, chlorella or spirulina, calcium and other minerals.

For poor circulation, proper exercise is essential, along with cayenne pepper, lecithin, sea kelp and seaweeds, and possibly some ginseng for men (preferably North American varieties for North Americans) or dong quai for women. For stress, B vitamins, vitamin C and magnesium are particularly helpful.

Many vegans seem to have trouble with extreme "cravings" which are often due to protein, calcium, B-12 or other vitamin and mineral deficiencies. These and other nutrient needs can be looked after by using the varied, nutritious foods and menus found in this book. See also the **Nutrient Guide for Vegans** following this article for a list of the main nutrients that vegans may be missing and the foods that supply them.

Although not everyone is aware of it, refined white sugar is *not* a vegan food! During the process of refining it, the sugar is often mixed with blood albumen from pigs and cattle and the granulated sugar may be filtered through charcoaled animal bones in a "purification" process.

Some vegans also avoid the use of honey, while others enjoy honey. The recipes in this book exclude honey as some vegans prefer not to use products taken from bees as they are often mistreated in the honey-making process. Today, some bees are fed sugar water so that all their honey can be taken for human consumption. This shortens the bees' life span and may lower the quality of the honey. Those who wish to include honey in their diet may prefer to purchase it from local beekeepers who care for their bees and allow them to eat some of their own honey.

I wish to applaud vegans everywhere for taking a stand for their health and the planet. It is my sincere hope that this book will be of immense benefit to vegans and encourage everyone to enjoy vegan foods until they are the preferred diet for all. I believe we are all headed for this diet eventually and it is important to make the switch a comfortable, easy one.

Everyone can enjoy these vegan delights! They are delicious gourmet treats that *any* good food lover will find satisfying. These recipes can be savoured and treasured—now and always.

Raise a toast to planet earth—be it carrot juice, almond milk or wine without the alcohol! Let us take care of our health and our land.

May your life be blessed!

JEANNE MARIE MARTIN

16

Nutrient Guide for Vegans

Make sure to enjoy these vitamin- and mineral-rich foods in your diet every day or as indicated for optimum health:

High-Protein Foods
Include 2–3 servings a day:

Soybeans	Tofu
Chick peas (garbanzos)	Almonds
Kidney beans	Other nuts and seeds
Adzuki beans	Amaranth
Other beans	Kamut and spelt
Mung beans	Other whole grains
Lentils	Peanuts

High-Calcium Foods
Include 2–4 servings a day:

Black beans (turtle beans)	Molasses
Chick peas (garbanzos)	Dark leafy green vegetables
Soybeans	Wakame/seaweeds
Pinto beans	Brazil nuts
Tofu	Hazelnuts (filberts)
Cashews	Sunflower seeds
Almonds	Sea kelp
Sesame seeds, sesame tahini	Globe artichokes

High-Magnesium Foods
Include 2–4 servings a day:

Pumpkin and squash seeds
Bran
Almonds
Sesame seeds
Other nuts and seeds
Peanuts

Millet
Whole grains
Dried figs
Molasses
Black-eyed peas
Sea kelp

High-Iron Foods
Include 1–2 servings a day:

Dried fruit
Molasses
Chick peas (garbanzos)
Black-eyed peas
Pinto beans
Whole grains

Sesame seeds
Other seeds
Prune juice
Dark leafy greens
Jerusalem artichokes

High-Zinc Foods
Include daily:

Brazil nuts
Bran
Almonds
Walnuts
Lentils
Lima beans
Black-eyed peas
Other dried peas

Chick peas (garbanzos)
Cashews
Pecans
Whole wheat flour
Corn and cornmeal
Spinach
Asparagus

High-Iodine Foods
Eat daily:

Seaweeds
Sea kelp

Iodized sea salt
Dark green leafy vegetables

High-Mineral and -Enzyme Foods
Include several servings a week:

Miso
Vegetable juices
Barley green
Wheat grass
Papayas
Seaweeds

Sauerkraut
Other lactic acid fermented
vegetables
Citrus fruit
Tomato juice

High-B12 Foods
Eat frequently:

Wheat grass
Barley green
Spirulina
Chlorella
Blue-green algae

Some nutritional yeasts
B12-fortified foods like T.V.P.
(texturized vegetable protein)
Vitamin supplements

Vitamin D
Eat frequently:

sunshine
alfalfa
chlorella
blue-green algae
fenugreek

some nutritional yeast
sunflower seeds
coconut
papaya
rosehips

Essential Oils
Include some every day:

Flax seed and/or oil

Olives

Olive oil

Other natural oils

Nuts and seeds

Vegetables

Avocados

Whole grains

Herbs
Eat frequently:

Parsley

Herb seasonings

Herb teas

Garlic

Onions

These are the nutrients vegans are sometimes deficient in. Other nutrients not mentioned on this chart are supplied by a balanced diet. Check the **Meal Planning Guidelines**, page 23.

Food Combining

Food combining is a rather complex issue as there are many conflicting points of view. I am convinced that certain combinations of food aid good digestion and help to assist in the healing process. I have found it invaluable in working with allergy sufferers, cancer patients and those with other health challenges. The two most important food combining principles are:

1. Eat heavy proteins (animal products) separately from carbohydrate foods. A simple thing for vegans to do, as it is okay to eat legumes and whole grains together.

2. Eat raw fruit alone or before a meal so as not to hinder digestion. The enzymes in raw fruit make them the easiest foods to digest, but upset stomach, indigestion and fermentation of stomach contents may occur if raw fruit is eaten with other foods or after a meal. Cooked fruit is like most other carbohydrate foods and is okay to eat after a meal.

Other special points:

1. Do not eat citrus fruit with grains as it makes them feel heavy as lead in the system and may increase the absorption of calories.

2. Eat desserts one hour or more after a full meal of other foods to lessen their effect on the body's blood sugar level and to decrease calorie absorption. Don't eat desserts on an empty stomach.

3. Vegetarians especially should not overeat sweets. It creates an imbalance in the system and may cause cravings for alcohol and

non-vegan foods. (It is preferable for vegans to avoid alcohol or indulge sparingly.)

4. Eat raw vegetables first in a meal to help stimulate and assist digestion. Chew foods well to mix lots of saliva with them and assist the digestive process.

5. Eat "grounding foods" if your mental energy gets scattered easily. Enjoy lots of cooked legumes, warm whole grains and warm cooked vegetables. Also eat some nut butters, tofu and seaweeds.

6. Most fruits and vegetables should not be eaten together at the same meal. Exceptions: apples—okay with most vegetables; citrus fruit—okay with salads (helps digestion); avocado (a fruit)—good with fruit or vegetables.

7. Don't mix too many foods together at one meal. Avoid 5-, 7- and 9-grain breads—they are hard to digest. Sometimes simple is better. Avoid heavy foods late at night.

8. Beverages should *generally* be taken without other foods, preferably ½–1 hour before or after a meal. Too much liquid may interfere with digestion, but 4–6 oz. is sometimes okay with a meal, taken in small sips as needed.

9. *Always* follow the suggestions that work best for you and suit your individual needs. Certain body types and health problems require variations of or omission of these tips. Consult your health specialist for diet changes as needed.

Meal Planning Guidelines

1. These menus need not be followed exactly. They are samples of nutritious meals, guidelines to planning meals and snacks that include all the vitamins, minerals and nutrients your body requires. Create your own menus in similar fashion.

2. For more economical meals, serve the same dish 2–4 times per week or freeze some leftovers for meals in later weeks. For convenience, make large batches of bean soups, chili, stews, burgers, balls, sauces, falafel and humus and freeze extra to defrost later for quick meals. Most tofu and legume foods keep up to 3 months frozen. Try cooking big batches one night during the week and/or one afternoon on weekends.

3. If you are allergic to or dislike any food, substitute another similar food in that recipe, or simply choose a selection from a different menu.

4. When creating your own menus, make sure not to plan too many light or heavy foods in one day. For example, with a dry cereal breakfast, try to have a hot, heavier lunch.

5. Make sure lunches and suppers include a whole grain, legume (beans, peas or lentils) and/or tofu dish.

6. About 50 percent of foods should be eaten raw and 50 percent cooked by the *average* person. In warm weather the proportion of raw may be increased to 75 percent or more, in cool weather you may want to eat fewer raw foods, perhaps as little as 25 percent. Cooked foods are very beneficial to many North American body types. Some nutrients are released and better

assimilated in cooked or warm foods like whole grains, legumes, carrots, winter squash and other foods. Some vegetables and other foods are more nutritious eaten raw. Include both raw and cooked foods in the diet for optimum health for the *average* person. Follow a diet plan that suits your body best!

Also see the **Food Combining** and **Food Preparation** sections for more information on proper meal planning.

Servings:

7. Enjoy 2–3 meals per day along with a few snacks if desired. Some people function better with two meals a day and some with three. If you wish to avoid breakfast or lunch, make sure to eat at least one of these meals by 12:00 noon.

8. Do not eat any one type of food more than 5–6 days per week. It is better to have two servings of a food every other day than to have one serving every day. Rotate foods for better digestion and health and to help prevent possible food allergies later in life.

9. Include weekly: 3–10 servings of legumes, 5–12 servings of *warm* whole grains, 2–5 servings of tofu. Enjoy nuts and seeds 3–5 days a week, and different vegetables may be eaten every day.

10. Include daily: 3–6 servings of vegetables (2 of green vegetables), 3–6 servings of carbohydrates (whole grains, cereals, starchy vegetables and pasta) and 2–3 servings of higher protein foods (legumes, tofu, nuts and seeds). Fruit needs vary. See **Fruit** below.

11. A serving is: 1 piece or 1 cup fruit, ½–1 cup cooked vegetables, 1 cup raw vegetables, ½–1 cup legumes or whole grains, 3–4 oz. (about 100 g) tofu, 2–4 Tbsp. nuts, seeds or nut/seed butters.

12. Add nutritious extras to sauces, whole grains and legumes at the table *after* cooking. Sprinkle 1/16–1/8 tsp. or less of sea kelp, dulse or cayenne, ¼–1 tsp. barley green or powdered spirulina, ½–1 tsp. ground flax seed or ground nuts or seeds, 1–5 tsp. nutritious oils (like flax or pumpkin), ¼–1 piece nori seaweed, toasted—whole or crumbled.

Fruit:

13. For proper food combining, always eat raw fruit 15–60 minutes *before* other foods (30 minutes is best).

14. Raw fruit may be enjoyed for snacks by itself during the day. Avoid eating raw fruit at night. Avoid eating tropical fruits too often in cold weather.

15. Cooked fruits do not contain certain enzymes found in raw fruit that mix poorly with other foods, so most cooked fruits may be eaten like other carbohydrates. Cooked fruits like apples and berries may be eaten with some meals or even after supper as a dessert.

16. Dried fruits should be eaten like fresh fruits. Eat them raw before meals and cooked with or after a meal.

17. Melons or grapes should be eaten by themselves. Citrus fruit may be eaten alone, or with vegetable salads to assist digestion. It is best not to eat them with other fruits.

18. Fruits may be interchanged in or eliminated from the menu for certain health concerns. (If you have blood sugar problems or Candida, avoid sweet fruit.) Enjoy fruit several times a week or up to 2–4 servings per day.

Snacks and Desserts:

19. Choose your own snacks, salad dressings and desserts to supplement these menus.

20. Snack suggestions: fresh fruit pieces, vegetable sticks alone or with a sauce or dip, nuts or seeds, tahini and celery, puffed wheat or rice cakes with toppings, bread or crackers with or without nut or seed butters, **Brown Rice Breakfast Chews**, muffins or quick breads, juices, "milks," **Granola** or other cereals, leftover balls or burgers. See also the **Snacks, Spreads, Dips** chapter. A few of the desserts are also good snacks, like the **Rice and Raisin Pudding**.

21. Enjoy desserts 3–6 times a week or less often. There is no real need for desserts in the diet, but they are enjoyable treats and anyone who is reasonably healthy and maintains a basic, balanced diet can afford to indulge in them once in a while.

22. Desserts are best served 1 hour after a meal, 1½–2 hours after a very large meal. Raw fruits should never be served as dessert, although it is all right to eat them *before* a meal. For example, fresh berries eaten 15 minutes or more before supper are okay occasionally.

23. After a light meal, choose a heavier dessert like cake, pie or pudding. After a heavy meal, light desserts like ice cream or a couple of cookies are recommended.

Remember:

24. *No* rule must be followed all the time! These are safe, wholesome guidelines for better digestion and health. A healthy individual need only follow these points *most* of the time! Basic rule: follow the guidelines carefully and eat *better* quality foods and eat less when not feeling well. Splurge or break the rules when you feel good. Each individual's needs will vary throughout their lives. Seek authoritative nutritional counselling for special needs and problems.

*NOTE: Fasting, cleansing, weight-loss or weight-gain, allergy and healing diets are not included in this book.

Sample Menus

Recipes named in **bold face type** appear in this book. Check the index.

SPRING

Monday

PRE-BREAKFAST FRUIT
Orange or ½ Grapefruit

BREAKFAST
Millet-Fruit Squares

LUNCH
Quick & Tasty Bean Balls or Pâté
Bread, Pita or Crackers
Raw vegetable sticks

SUPPER
Bravo Burritos
Guacamole
Chopped red tomatoes and
  vegetables
Optional: Whole grain dish

Thursday

PRE-BREAKFAST FRUIT
Pear or other basic fruit

BREAKFAST
Rice-ola *or* Steamed carrots with
  nut or seed sauce

LUNCH
Kamut Nut or **Spelt Burgers** (can
  be defrosted)
Natural Ketchup, sauce or gravy
Bun, whole wheat or rye bread

SUPPER
Spinach Salad
Marinated Broiled Tofu Strips
Broccoli or Brussels sprouts with
  Easy Lemon Sauce *or* **Spring
  Green Onion Soup**

Friday

PRE-BREAKFAST FRUIT
Apple or banana

BREAKFAST
Brown Rice Breakfast Chews *or*
  Rice and Raisin Pudding

LUNCH
T.V.P. or **Lentil Vegetable
  Goulash**
Country Cornbread

SUPPER
Romaine Salad
Pasta
Tomato or **Mock Tomato Sauce** *or*
  Vegan, Easy Pesto or
  Kind-of-a-Pesto Sauce

Tuesday

PRE-BREAKFAST FRUIT

2–3 Kiwi fruits

BREAKFAST

Granola or dry cereal with fruit juice or milk substitute *or* Whole grain toast with jam

LUNCH

Pita Pizzas or **Pizza Breads**

SUPPER

Early Green Salad
Japanese Brown Rice Sushi *or* Kasha Pilaf
Steamed vegetables
Toasted Sesame *or* **Cashew Sauce**

Wednesday

PRE-BREAKFAST FRUIT

None–cooked fruit in cereal

BREAKFAST

Cornmeal *or* **Hot Millet Cereal** with raisins or dried fruit

LUNCH

Seaweed Soup *or* **Hearty Vegetable Soup** *or* Leftover **Bravo Burritos** with corn chips, crackers or whole wheat pretzels

SUPPER

Of Radishes and Things Salad
Celebration Cabbage Rolls
Tomato or **Mock Tomato Sauce** or **Mushroom Gravy**

Saturday

PRE-BREAKFAST FRUIT

Orange, grapefruit or lemon juice

BREAKFAST

Scrambled Tofu
Whole grain toast with **Veggie Butter**

LUNCH

Leftover **Hearty Vegetable Soup** *or* **Seaweed Soup**
Essene bread, **Soda Bread** or other bread

SUPPER

Avocado Boats *or* Avocado stuffed with **Marinated Vegetable Medley**
Spinach Tofu Calzones
Tomato or **Mock Tomato Sauce** *or* **Mock Cheese Sauce**

Sunday

PRE-BREAKFAST FRUIT

Strawberries or other berries

BREAKFAST

Pancakes with applesauce or cooked fruit

LUNCH

Stir-Fried Vegetables with Whole Grains
Add **Tempeh**

SUPPER

Classic Green Salad
Vegan Roast
Vegetarian or **Mushroom Gravy** or **Arrowroot Sauce**
Baked or steamed yams or potatoes
Amazing Artichokes *or* asparagus with **Citrus Sauce 1** or **2**

SUMMER

Monday

PRE-BREAKFAST FRUIT
Peach or nectarine

BREAKFAST
Rice and Raisin Pudding *or*
 Brown Rice Breakfast Chews

LUNCH
Garden Vegetable Soup
Country Cornbread *or* **Essene**
 bread
Royal Snack Mix

SUPPER
Beet Treat Salad
Lentil Burgers
Bread, corn chips or crackers

Thursday

PRE-BREAKFAST FRUIT
Plum or pear

BREAKFAST
Cold or hot **Quinoa Cereal** with
 jam

LUNCH
Easy Tamari Tofu Sauté *and/or*
 Leftover **Wonderful Millet**
 Vegetable Balls
Raw vegetable sticks

SUPPER
Italian Pasta Salad
Quick Zucchini Soup *or* **Easy**
 Asparagus Soup
Quick Garlic Bread

Friday

PRE-BREAKFAST FRUIT
Cantaloupe or other melon

BREAKFAST
Granola or other dry cereal

LUNCH
Tomato-Rice Soup
Spinach-Tofu Dip
Whole wheat or other whole grain
 bread

SUPPER
Wild Greens Salad *or* **Romaine**
 Salad
Savoury Sloppy Jo's with buns

Tuesday

PRE-BREAKFAST FRUIT

Berries

BREAKFAST

Oatmeal with cooked dried fruit

LUNCH

Tangy Stuffed Tomatoes with **Humus, Falafel** or **Mock Tofu Egg Salad**

SUPPER

Greek Salad

Wonderful Millet Vegetable Balls

Cooked dark leafy greens: kale, chard, spinach, mustard or collard with **Avocado Sauce** or **Creamy Cashew Sauce**

Wednesday

PRE-BREAKFAST FRUIT

Pineapple or orange or grapefruit

BREAKFAST

Zucchini-Carrot Bread or Muffins

LUNCH

Perfect Potato Salad *or* **8 Layer Mexican Dip** with corn chips

SUPPER

Classic Green Salad

Fantastic Fondues

Saturday

PRE-BREAKFAST FRUIT

Exotic fruit: mango, papaya, persimmon or other

BREAKFAST

Tofu French Toast with cooked fruit or applesauce

LUNCH

Mushroom and Tomato Stuffed Peppers

Flatbreads, pita or crackers

SUPPER

Oriental Salad

Hot and Sour Soup *or* **Miso Soup**

Broiled Tamari Vegetables served over cooked whole grain

Sunday

PRE-BREAKFAST FRUIT

Orange or grapefruit

BREAKFAST

Millet-Fruit Parfaits

LUNCH

Leftover **Savoury Sloppy Jo's**

Marinated Vegetable Medley on a bed of chopped greens

SUPPER

Flowers and Wild Greens Salad

Tofu Rarebit

AUTUMN

Monday

PRE-BREAKFAST FRUIT
Grapes

BREAKFAST
Sweet Brown Rice Cereal *or* Hot Millet Cereal

LUNCH
Easy Sunflower Pâté *or* Hazelnut Pâté
Rye or whole wheat crackers or bread
Garden Snack Mix

SUPPER
Classic Green Salad with alfalfa sprouts
Beet Treat
Italian Style Beans
Baked/Glazed or /Herb Turnips or Yams

Thursday

PRE-BREAKFAST FRUIT
Cherries or plums

BREAKFAST
Rice-ola *or* Granola *or* Zucchini-Carrot Muffins *or* Beautiful Banana Bread *or* Banana Nut Rice Bread

LUNCH
Oat Nut Burgers
Seaweed Soup *or* Hearty Vegetable Soup

SUPPER
Squash Apple Soup
8 Layer Mexican Dip
Corn chips

Friday

PRE-BREAKFAST FRUIT
Dried fruit

BREAKFAST
Baked squash with **Home Roasted Nuts**

LUNCH
Tangy Stuffed Tomatoes with Humus, Falafel or Mock Tofu Egg Salad

SUPPER
Avocado Boats *or* Avocado stuffed with **Marinated Vegetable Medley**
Molasses and Beans Hot Pot
Baked Potato or Turnip Fries

Sample Menus

Tuesday

PRE-BREAKFAST FRUIT
Raspberries, blackberries or other
berries

BREAKFAST
Easy Tamari Tofu Sauté with a
nut sauce or **Stuffed Canneloni
or Conchiglie**
Green vegetables

LUNCH
Pita Pizzas or **Pizza Breads** or
Spanish Vegetable Paella

SUPPER
Great Grated Salad
Celebration Cabbage Rolls
Tomato or **Mock Tomato Sauce**

Wednesday

PRE-BREAKFAST FRUIT
Honeydew melon

BREAKFAST
Leftover **Sweet Brown Rice
Cereal** or Hot **Millet Cereal**

LUNCH
Olive and Nut Dip and/or **Carrot
Tofu Dip**
Raw vegetable sticks
Essene bread

SUPPER
Greek Salad
Orange Yam Sauce or **Sweet
Onion Sauce**
Steamed or sautéed vegetables
Cooked whole grain
Nori

Saturday

PRE-BREAKFAST FRUIT
Watermelon

BREAKFAST
Cornmeal with raisins or currants

LUNCH
Tangy T.V.P. with Sauces
(**Creamy Garlic, Tahini** or other)
Steamed vegetables
Cooked whole grain

SUPPER
Wild Zucchini Rice Salad
Quick Broccoli Soup or **Healing
Greens Soup**
**Spanish Mushrooms in Garlic
Sauce**
Country Cornbread, Essene bread
or **Soda Bread**

Sunday

PRE-BREAKFAST FRUIT
Orange or grapefruit or pineapple

BREAKFAST
Whole Grain Pancakes or **Scrambled
Tofu** with whole grain toast

LUNCH
Mild Curry Dip
Vegetable sticks
Leftover soup
Flatbreads or pita

SUPPER
Spinach Salad
Easy or **Elegant Chestnut Soup** or
Magnificent Mushroom Soup
Tofu "Meatballs" with **Tomato** or
Mock Tomato Sauce
Cinnamon Baked Squash

WINTER

Monday

PRE-BREAKFAST FRUIT
Pear

BREAKFAST
Amaranth or **Quinoa Cereal**

LUNCH
Humus
Pita or **Flatbreads**
Raw vegetable sticks or hot/cold
  steamed vegetables

SUPPER
Super Sprout Salad
Millet, Rice or Quinoa Burgers
  with **Natural Ketchup** and extras
  or gravy
Bun or bread

Thursday

PRE-BREAKFAST FRUIT
Pineapple or citrus fruit

BREAKFAST
Cooked **Oat Groats** *or* **Whole Oats**
  or **Spelt**

LUNCH
Leftover **Cornucopia Soup**
Easy Sunflower Pâté or **Hazelnut
Pâté**
Rye or wheat crackers or bread

SUPPER
Bravo Burritos with chopped
  vegetables
Guacamole

Friday

PRE-BREAKFAST FRUIT
Papaya or winter melon

BREAKFAST
Oatmeal *or* **Sweet Brown Rice
Cereal**

LUNCH
Leftover **Tangy T.V.P. and Bean
Chili**
Raw vegetable sticks

SUPPER
Romaine Salad
Tofu or **T.V.P. Vegetable Balls or
Burgers**
Spicy Nut Sauce or **Gado Gado
Spicy Peanut Sauce**
Steamed or sautéed vegetables
Cooked whole grain

Tuesday

PRE-BREAKFAST FRUIT
Kiwis

BREAKFAST
Hot **Millet Cereal** *or* **Oatmeal**

LUNCH
Cornucopia Soup
Wild Zucchini Rice Salad
Nori

SUPPER
Of Radishes and Things Salad
Tangy T.V.P. and Bean Chili
Whole grain, **Country Cornbread**
  or **Essene bread**

Wednesday

PRE-BREAKFAST FRUIT
Apple or banana

BREAKFAST
Millet-Fruit Squares *or* **Brown**
  Rice Breakfast Chews

LUNCH
Kamut Nut Burgers (can be
  defrosted) with **Natural**
  Ketchup, tamari or gravy
Corn or potato chips, crackers or
  natural pretzels

SUPPER
Beet Treat Salad
Adzuki or Pinto Bean Soup
Broiled Tamari Vegetables
Flatbreads, pita or crackers

Saturday

PRE-BREAKFAST FRUIT
Orange, grapefruit or lemon juice

BREAKFAST
Baked squash with **Home Roasted**
  Nuts *or* **Scrambled Tofu**

LUNCH
Potato Salad *or* **Tofu Rarebit**

SUPPER
Spinach Salad with alfalfa sprouts
Vegan Roast
Vegetarian or **Mushroom Gravy**
Parsley and Rice Casserole

Sunday

PRE-BREAKFAST FRUIT
Japanese apples or pear/apples or
  other exotic fruit

BREAKFAST
Tofu French Toast with cooked
  berries or applesauce

LUNCH
Leftover **Bravo Burritos** with
  Guacamole *or* Leftover **Parsley**
  and Rice Casserole with
  chopped vegetables

SUPPER
Millet or Quinoa Salad
Vegetable Bean Casserole
Stir-Fried Vegetables (without the
  whole grains)

Food Preparation: Saving Energy

As much as 90 per cent of the nutrients and energy in food may be lost by the time it reaches your dinner plate. Food growing conditions, transporting, storage, improper handling, processing and refining, poor selection and home preparation techniques, and under- and overcooking can all diminish the value of our foods. To help preserve more nutrients—vitamins, minerals and "life energy"—follow these tips whenever possible:

1. Buy *good* quality, certified organic foods when available and reasonably priced. Avoid spoiled, underripe or heavily damaged organic foods.

2. Grow your own organic produce or buy good quality, local, organic produce whenever possible. (If you grow your own, you may want to get your soil checked for heavy metals and other pollutants before you plant.)

3. Pick garden foods just before the meal to preserve vitamins and flavours.

4. Learn to choose the freshest foods, wisely. Selecting good produce is an art. Shop for quality brand names and products that do not harm the environment. Check suppliers when you can. Check produce for softness/firmness, smell, texture, shape, colours, bruises and blemishes.

5. Store foods at proper temperatures to maintain freshness (see **Maximum Storage Temperatures**, page 43).

6. Don't leave produce soaking in water—that drains nutrients. Wash and prepare raw foods quickly before each meal. Special vegetable cleaners can be purchased in health food stores to add to washing water to help remove pollutants like chemical sprays and preservatives.

7. Don't discard valuable edible skins and seeds of some foods. Include skins in mashed potatoes and leaves and stalks on broccoli. (Peel broccoli stalks for best digestion.)

8. Make sure foods are fully ripe before using. Unripe produce lacks vitamins and flavour. Overripe fruit can have too high a sugar and/or mold content. Moldy produce can contribute to Candida Albicans, stomach upset and other illnesses.

9. Don't cook on too high a heat or cook foods any longer than necessary. But don't undercook either—this makes foods hard to digest, especially some vegetables, whole grains and legumes.

10. Don't reheat leftovers more than once. After more than two heatings, foods have lost most of their nutrients and flavour but not their calories. Only cook as much as you can eat and safely store.

Food and Cooking Tips

1. ¾ tsp. sea salt equals 1 tsp. regular table salt. (Regular table salt contains sugar!) Sea salt is the healthier choice.

2. For low-salt diets, sea salt amounts may be decreased in recipes *except* bread and cake recipes. Reduce amounts, taste, and add more salt as desired.

3. When doubling a recipe only use 1½ times the amount of salt. When tripling a recipe—double the salt.

4. When oil is used in recipes, try a natural variety. (See **About Oils**, page 48). As with all natural oil products (including mayonnaise and salad dressings), refrigerate after opening. This is a must for safety and freshness!

5. To prevent early spoilage of liquid foods (oil, mayonnaise, dressings, etc.), avoid contaminating them by adding saliva or perspiration, or overexposing them to air. Avoid eating any part of fruits, vegetables, breads or other foods on which mold has begun to grow. Discard any food that may not be fresh.

6. Kelp (sea kelp) is an important food supplement. It contains iodine and other minerals and sea salt contains no iodine so kelp and sea salt are almost always used together. Kelp also adds flavour and gives body and depth to recipes. Enjoy it often for its many benefits. Avoid using too much or a recipe may taste "muddy."

7. All nuts and seeds called for in these recipes are raw unless specified otherwise. All nuts and seeds should be chewed very well for good digestion. Chew them to powder to mix in lots of saliva.

8. All types of carbohydrate juices like vegetable and

non-acidic fruit juices should be sipped very slowly and even swished in the mouth before swallowing to aid digestion and absorption of nutrients. Never gulp juices, savour them. Avoid keeping citrus juices in the mouth, as they may begin to strip the enamel from the teeth.

9. In recipes that call for parsley, basil, oregano or other herbs, the quantities shown are for dried herbs. Fresh chopped herbs should be added only when specified. In some recipes, fresh and dried herbs may be interchanged. Use 2-5 tsp. dried herbs per ¼ cup fresh herbs.

10. Use real vanilla flavouring in all recipes for uncooked foods and for cooked foods if desired. It is preferable to use real vanilla extract when ingredients are heated, cooked or baked. The extract contains alcohol.

11. Equal amounts of honey may be used instead of maple syrup or fruit concentrate in recipes if desired.

12. Purchased soy yogurt or flavoured soft tofu may be used instead of dairy yogurt to accompany some recipes.

13. To keep dates from sticking when you cut them, oil your knife or scissors.

14. To measure maple syrup or liquid sweeteners, first measure the oil for the recipe in the same cup, or oil the cup before measuring. The sweetener will slip out easily.

15. Add 2-3 tsp. instant coffee substitute to carob recipes for a more chocolate-like flavour.

16. Equal amounts of unsweetened cocoa powder may be used instead of carob powder in recipes if desired. Carob is lower in fats and calories and does not contain caffeine.

17. All of the ingredients found in this book are available at local markets, health food stores or ethnic shops. If you have trouble finding any specific items, or if you need more information about the special ingredients called for in these recipes, check the glossary and buying guide in *The All Natural Allergy Cookbook*.

Baking Tips

1. To prevent bread dough from sticking to a baking pan, lightly oil the inside bottom and sides of the pan. Make sure the oil does not run. If necessary, lightly wipe out excess with paper towelling. Then shake flour all around the inside of the pan, shake out the excess and tap the pan lightly so that only a thin coating remains. For yeast breads, shape the dough outside of the pan and place it in the oiled and floured pan to rise. For quick breads, scoop the batter into the pan and spread evenly. Loosen the bread with a table knife 10–15 minutes after baking, and it will slide from the pan easily.

2. To keep cakes from sticking to the pan, use the method described above for breads. *Or,* oil the bottom of the pan, line it with waxed paper and oil the waxed paper. After baking, loosen the sides of the cake with a table knife, turn the cake upside-down on a rack and peel off the waxed paper.

3. When baking, make sure baking pans are at least 1 inch from each other and from the sides of the oven. If two racks are used, do not place one pan directly above the other.

4. To avoid fallen cakes and quick breads, try not to open the oven door or jostle the pan until the cake or bread is nearly done.

5. To test a cake or a quick bread (baking powder bread) for doneness, insert a toothpick into the middle of the cake. It will come out clean when the cake is done. A cake or bread may look completely baked in the oven, but it may still be raw inside. Be sure not to remove the cake from the oven while testing, or it will

stop baking and remain uncooked inside—even with further baking time!

6. For maximum flavour, serve freshly baked cakes and breads at room temperature.

Abbreviations, Measurements, Symbols, Metric Equivalents

ABBREVIATIONS

tsp.	teaspoon	oz.	ounce
Tbsp.	tablespoon	g.	gram
lb.	pound		

MEASUREMENTS

3 tsp. = 1 Tbsp.

4 Tbsp. = ¼ cup

8 Tbsp. = ½ cup

16 Tbsp. = 1 cup

1 oz. = 2 Tbsp.

4 oz. = ½ cup

8 oz. = 1 cup

RECIPE SYMBOLS

* variation

Recipes named in **boldface type** appear in this book.
Check the index.

METRIC EQUIVALENTS (approximate)

¼ tsp.	1 mL	¾ cup	180 mL
½ tsp.	2 mL	1 cup	250 mL
1 tsp.	5 mL	1 pt.	500 mL
1 Tbsp.	15 mL	1 qt.	1 L
¼ cup	60 mL	4 oz.	115 g
⅓ cup	75 mL	8 oz.	225 g
½ cup	125 mL	1 lb.	450 g

Maximum Storage Temperatures for Staple Vegan Foods

Grains and beans	62°F
Flours and meals	55°F
Hard fruits	Room temperature
Fresh vegetables and soft fruits	45°F
Root vegetables	60°F
Dried fruit	65°F
Frozen food	0°F
Natural oil products	35°F

Special Foods

SWEETENERS

The amount of sweetener called for in a recipe may be altered to suit your own taste. If you like less sweetener, add less. A recipe can be made sweeter by reducing the amount of flour by about 1/4–1/2 cup and adding the same amount of powdered or granulated sweetener. Maple syrup or other sweetener may be substituted for honey in most recipes from other books.

Fruit concentrates may be used in place of honey or maple syrup, in about equal proportions.

Regular fruit juice may be used as a sole sweetening agent in some recipes, with small variations in flavour. For example, if a recipe calls for 2 cups maple syrup and 1½ cups nut milk, use 3½ cups of a thick variety of peach or pear juice (other fruit juices are not as sweet or light-coloured). There will be a slight change in flavour. If a recipe using only fruit juice is not sweet enough, substitute ½ cup or so of one of the recipe's dry ingredients (like flour) with the same amount of a natural powdered or granulated sweetener.

When a recipe calls for a liquid sweetener, it is best to use maple syrup, fruit concentrate or natural liquid sweetener for the best flavour. If any other liquid sweeteners are used, the amount of sweetening may be increased. Some sweeteners, like molasses or sorghum, can greatly change the flavour of a recipe and must be experimented with.

Alternative Sweeteners

amazake (rice culture sweetener)
maple syrup
maple sugar
brown date sugar
molasses
fructose
date spread
fruit sugar (unrefined)
fruit butter
fruit juice
fruit concentrate
fruit juice concentrate
honeyleaf (stevia)
natural raw sugar (SUCANAT®)
sorghum
barley malt powder and syrup
natural granular sweetener (FRUITSOURCE®)
natural liquid sweetener (FRUITSOURCE®)
rice syrup

THICKENERS

COLD FOODS:

For *cold* foods, like salad dressings, ice creams, gelatin substitutes, puddings:

What to use: Guar gum, xanthan gum, other gums.

How to use: Use blender, electric mixer or food processor to mix with other ingredients and thicken almost instantly.

How much to use: 1–2 tsp. powdered gum per recipe (about 1 loaf of bread, 1 cake or 2 cups liquid).

HOT FOODS

For *hot* foods, like gravies, sauces, stews, soups, heated puddings, breads, baked desserts:

What to use: Guar gum, xanthan gum, arrowroot (see below), agar agar powder (see below).

How to use: In *dry* ingredients, mix thoroughly with other ingredients before baking. In *liquids*, mix in cold liquid, heat and stir until thickened. Let cool to set.

How much to use: 1–3 tsp. powdered thickener per recipe (about 1 loaf of bread, 1 cake or up to 1 quart liquid).

OTHER THICKENERS

Agar agar: Use about 1–2 tsp. powder or 2–6 tsp. flakes to thicken 1–2 cups liquid. Mix with cool liquid and heat slowly, stirring, until thickened. Strain and add to recipe.

Arrowroot: Use ½–1 tsp. to thicken 1 cup liquid. Mix with cool liquid and heat slowly, stirring until thickened. Remove from heat or add to recipe.

Kudzu: To use kudzu as a thickener, 1 tsp. kudzu = 3 tsp. flour; 2 tsp. kudzu = 3 tsp. arrowroot.

Use 1–2 tsp. kudzu to thicken 1 cup soup or sauce.

Use 1–2 Tbsp. kudzu per cup for jello or jelled desserts.

Crush the powdered chunks in cold liquid, mash and dissolve well. Strain and heat to thicken.

EGG SUBSTITUTES

Liquid lecithin is used in some recipes instead of eggs. It is best if used along with 2 tsp. guar gum. Experiment with lecithin and guar gum in other recipes.

A powdered egg substitute can also be purchased to replace eggs in many bread and cake recipes. It is best to use a bit more egg replacer than the package may suggest. For *each* egg omitted, use 2–3 tsp. powdered egg replacer added to the dry ingredients, and 3½ Tbsp. water or other liquid added to the wet ingredients.

You can make your own egg substitute to use as a binder, not a leavening agent. Combine ⅓ cup water and 3–4 tsp. brown flax seeds. Bring to a boil on high heat, then simmer on low heat for 5–7 minutes until a slightly thickened gel begins to form. Strain the flax seed out of the liquid and use the gel in recipes. This recipe makes enough substitute for 1 egg. Increase the amounts as needed to substitute for 2, 3 or more eggs. Some people prefer to leave the flax seeds in the mixture after thickening, or blend them into the gel before using. This may alter the recipe's taste a little.

ABOUT OILS

There is extensive controversy over which types of oils to use and why. It is not one of the purposes of this book to settle the dispute, but rather to shed a little light on the subject.

There are three basic processes for the manufacture of cooking oils. The first is the solvent extraction method by which most commercial and supermarket oils are obtained. Some harmful petroleum by-products like octane, heptane and hexane are mixed with mashed seeds, beans or nuts to assist in the extraction process and obtain greater quantities of oil. Then the oil and solvents are separated because the solvents are toxic. The oil extracted this way still contains some solvent residues. For obvious reasons, these oils are not recommended.

The second method is cold-pressed. No solvents are used, and lower pressing temperatures are maintained. By this method much less oil is extracted and the product becomes more expensive.

The third method is expeller-pressed. Even cooler pressing temperatures are maintained during this process. While cold-pressed oils may be refined to some degree, expeller-pressed oil is merely pressed. Organic nuts and seeds are often used to make expeller-pressed oils.

Expeller-pressed oil retains the most nutrients, including valuable Omega 3 and 6 essential fatty acids, and the strongest flavour. Some oils extracted this way, like flax seed (linseed) and pumpkin oil, are best if they are used only raw in salads and with mixed raw dishes. It is important to include one or both of these oils in a vegan diet to obtain the essential Omega 3 and 6. Another way to get these oils is to grind flax seeds and sprinkle them on cereals or whole grains, and over sauces and other foods at the table. Keep refrigerated after grinding for up to 1–2 weeks.

Most of the other expeller-pressed oils may be used in cooking, but they *must be experimented with* in recipes as they have a stronger flavour and some of them can overpower the other ingredients in a dish!

I sometimes prefer to use just cold-pressed oils in general cooking, even though they are less nutritious, as I can count on a mild flavour. These types of oils are generally lighter in colour. The best types of oil to cook with are the 3 S's: sesame, safflower and sunflower. (*Not* soy, which requires more processing and is less digestible.) Olive oil is also good for some recipes.

In this book I specify only "natural" oil and "natural light" oil. When a recipe calls for natural oil, you may use expeller-pressed oils. They taste good only if used in the right recipes! Experiment with them, or for more uniform taste use cold-pressed oils where "natural" oil is called for. In all the mild-tasting recipes and desserts, I recommend "natural light" oil. To be on the safe side I generally stick with cold-pressed oils for these, but I do use some expeller-pressed almond and walnut oils in some dessert recipes.

For other specialties, toasted sesame oil is the best flavour for stir-frys. Although it is expensive, very little is used at a time, so a little bottle lasts a while. Safflower, sunflower and olive oil are generally less expensive.

Keep *all* natural oils refrigerated after opening. Discard oils after the date on the label, if any, or after 3–6 months stored in the refrigerator after opening. Do not let perspiration, saliva or bacteria get into the oil bottle and don't let oil sit out of the fridge too long, especially on a hot day. Once oil is poured out of its bottle, never pour it back into the bottle as it may easily collect bacteria or dust once poured. Oil poisoning is very painful and dangerous!

For more information, see *Fats and Oils* by Udo Erasmus (Alive Books) or *Facts About Fats* by John Finnegan (Elysian Arts Books).

Some recommended expeller-pressed oils are Flora, Arrowhead Mills and Omega. Some recommended cold-pressed oils are Spectrum, Lifestream and Eden. Other good brand names may also be available. Check at your natural foods store.

ABOUT MARGARINE

When it comes to margarine, it should be avoided completely. Dr. Zoltan Rona, M.D. (author of *Joy of Health* from Hounslow Press) says: "Margarine is nothing more than plastic butter." Dr. Rudolph Ballantine, M.D. (author of *Diet and Nutrititon* from the Himalayan International Institute) says that the rise in heart disease directly parallels the rise in the use of margarine. He states: "It seems increasingly likely that eating margarine, instead of preventing heart attacks, actually accelerates the process which causes them."

ABOUT TOFU

Tofu is a wonderful meat or dairy substitute made from soy. It is low in calories and contains no cholesterol. 8 oz (about 225 g) of tofu provides: 164 calories, 17.6 g protein, 292 mg calcium (the same as 8 oz milk), 286 mg phosphorus, 96 mg potassium and as much iron as 4–5 eggs.

Although tofu is bland by itself, it works wonders in recipes as it absorbs the flavours of the ingredients around it and actually extends and complements the taste of sauces, gravies, herbs and spices. Used correctly, tofu is delicious and adds texture, protein and other nutrients to all types of dishes, including salads, main dishes, dressings, sauces and desserts.

Store tofu completely covered by fresh water, preferably in a glass jar, in the refrigerator. Plain tofu is fresh as long as it retains its milky white colour and has no scent or taste. If the tofu smells a bit, rinse it thoroughly. If no smell remains, it can still be cooked but should not be eaten "raw." If the tofu still has an odour *after* rinsing—discard it!

Whenever the freshness of tofu is questionable or to avoid any chance of bacteria growth, lightly steam it for 4–9 minutes before using it.

Soft, pressed, medium and firm or regular tofu are available. The soft tofu may be used in any dessert recipe for a less grainy texture. However, regular tofu may be used unless specified otherwise.

WHOLE GRAINS

Whole grains are delicious, nutritious and more digestible than refined grains when properly prepared. They are less likely to aggravate allergic conditions, low blood sugar, diabetes and Candida. They contain natural fibre and are lower in calories than many refined food products. There are cereal grains and main dish grains.

Special Tips on Whole Grains

1. Grains are generally cooked in 2 or more cups of water per 1 cup of grain.

2. Cook grains until they are no longer crunchy, but not soggy or mushy. Grains should be tender and easy to chew. Improperly cooked grains are extremely hard to digest!

3. Very few grains need to be soaked before cooking. These include wild rice (sometimes), whole oats, rye, triticale and wheat kernels (berries).

4. Raw rolled, flaked or crushed grains must be soaked before eating. Toasted grains may be eaten as they are or with milk substitutes or fruit juices (apple, pear and peach are excellent for this). They should be well chewed.

5. Before cooking, check grains for dirt balls, gravel, husks and other foreign particles by spreading them out thinly and fingering through them.

6. Brown rice and quinoa are usually the only grains that need prewashing, but you may wash any grain if you feel it needs it.

7. It makes little difference whether you start cooking a grain in cool or warm water. The exception is ground cereals, which get lumpy when put in warm water, unless mixed in carefully with a wire whisk.

8. To prevent grains from boiling over and to distribute heat evenly, water and grains together should never cover more than three-fourths of the cooking pot.

9. Do not add salt or oil to whole grains until the last 10–15 minutes of cooking, to make digestion easier.

10. Any grain in *whole* form (does not include rolled or broken whole grains) will never burn during its *first* cooking process as long as the water does not run out and the grain does not become overcooked to the point that it falls apart (this usually takes 1¼ hours or longer). Also, they must be cooked on low heat.

11. Never stir whole grains while cooking or they will stick and burn. Keep grains covered while cooking.

12. When reheating cooked whole grains, add ¼–⅓ cup extra water per cup of grain. Cook the grain, covered, on very low heat until warmed. Brown rice can be reheated by steaming in a vegetable steamer.

13. One cup of dry whole grain or cereal makes about 4 servings.

14. The main dish grains can almost always be substituted one for the other in different recipes, except for wild rice. Grains are similar, but may differ slightly in taste.

15. Wheat, rye, triticale, barley, oats, kamut and spelt contain gluten. Other grains contain minute amounts of gluten but are not considered gluten grains and are not usually eliminated from gluten-free diets.

Preparing Main Dish Grains

Natural buckwheat and pot barley. Use about 2 cups water per 1 cup grain. Bring the grain to a boil, then turn down the heat to a low bubble. Cover and simmer 20–30 minutes or until tender and no longer crunchy, adding extra water if needed. Cook onions with the grain, and add herbs and salt during the last 10 minutes of cooking time.

Kasha (toasted buckwheat). Cook the same as natural buckwheat, but use a bit less water and reduce the cooking time to 15–20 minutes.

Job's tears. Bring 2–3 cups water and 1 cup of the "seed" to a boil. Reduce the heat to a simmer (make sure there are small bubbles forming in the water) and cook for about 60 minutes or longer, until very tender. Serve with a sauce or vegetables as this is quite robust all by itself. It can also be mixed with other whole grains or used in soups, stews or casseroles instead of barley, buckwheat or brown rice.

Millet (main dish). Cook the same as rice, but use 2½ cups water per 1 cup dry millet. It usually does not need pre-washing. Simmer 40–55 minutes and use as a substitute for rice in rice dishes. This is one of the best grains, high in vitamins and very alkaline.

Quinoa. Rinse thoroughly before cooking by rubbing the grains together well in a pot of water and changing the water 2–4 times. This helps to remove the saponin, which may irritate digestion or allergies. Use 2–3 cups water to 1 cup quinoa and bring water and quinoa to a boil. Cover and simmer 20–25 minutes until tender. Add sea salt if desired. Use the cooked quinoa in place of rice or millet in main dishes.

Whole oats, whole triticale, whole wheat kernels (wheat berries—hard red or soft yellow) and **whole spelt**. These must be soaked in 2½ cups water per 1 cup oats for several hours or overnight before cooking. Then change the water and simmer for 45–60 minutes. The oats will be slightly chewy but not crunchy when done. Cook until tender for the best digestion. The grains can be cooked separately or with other whole grains.

Whole rye. Soak and cook the same as whole oats or spelt, above, but use it sparingly because it is strong and bitter. Mix it with oats or spelt in a ratio of 1 part rye to 6–10 parts oats or spelt, and cook them together. Rye adds zest to simple meals, but its flavour does not appeal to everyone.

Short- and long-grain brown rice. Put rice in a pot and fill it with water. Rub the rice together with your fingers and swish it around to remove extra starches, dirt and stray husks. Discard all the water. If the water was very cloudy during the first washing, repeat the process once or twice until the water is relatively clear. Put 2–2¼ cups water per 1 cup rice in the pot. Bring to a boil over medium heat, then cover, turn down the heat and simmer 45–60 minutes. When the rice is no longer crunchy but easy to chew and tender, not soggy, it is done. Onions, herbs and spices can be added during the last 15–20 minutes of cooking time. Keep the pot tightly covered while cooking, but it won't hurt to peek!

Wild rice. This is one of the few main dish grains that sometimes requires soaking before cooking. Wash and then soak 1 cup rice in 2 cups water for 2–4 hours. Only by experimenting can you find out whether your wild rice needs soaking. Many varieties can just be cooked, but if they are still hard after 1–1½ hours of cooking, turn off the heat, let them cool and cook them again until tender. Next time, pre-soak it! Then cook the rice as you would cook brown rice. Wild rice is very expensive and rich-tasting, so it is often mixed with brown rice for a delicious, light-tasting, less expensive dish. Use one part wild rice to 2–10 parts brown rice. Cook the two rices separately and mix before serving, or cook wild rice for 15–20 minutes, then add the brown rice to it and cook them together for 45–60 minutes longer. Add extra water if needed.

For information on preparing cereal grains, see **Breakfasts.**

LEGUMES: BEANS, PEAS AND LENTILS

Beans, beans, the musical fruit,
The more you eat, the more you toot.
The more you toot, the better you feel,
So eat your beans with every meal!

A wonder food of the new century will be beans! They were basically a forgotten food in North America until the last twenty years. Now, finally, people are discovering the tremendous value of beans. For flavour, versatility and nutritional value, beans are unsurpassed as a food source. With proper knowledge, one can create thousands of mouth-watering, taste-tempting, delicious bean dishes including soups, stews, sauces, salads, burgers, loafs, casseroles, breads and even desserts. Yes, desserts! Ever tried Pinto Bean Pumpkin Pie?

The beauty of beans is that they are chock-full of vitamins (especially B vitamins), protein and minerals like calcium, potassium, phosphorus and iron. Black-eyed peas are very high in magnesium. Some beans, like soybeans, chick peas, black beans and pinto beans, contain more calcium and iron per serving than some dairy products.

Beans may be a unique food for North Americans but they are common foods in the rest of the world. In Mexico, kidney beans and pinto beans, used in chili, burritos and tacos, are national favourites. In India, *dahl* made with red lentils or split peas is a staple. In the Mediterranean, chick peas are a mainstay in recipes for humus (hummous) and falafels. In Greece, brown lentil soups are traditional. In China, Japan and other Oriental countries, soybeans, in the form of tofu curd, are everyday foods. Even in the United States black-eyed peas are as popular in the South as baked beans are in the rest of the country.

Across the world, beans are enjoyed as wholesome, delicious foods that are a major part of everyday diets. North Americans may find this surprising, but more than three-quarters of the world's population is basically vegetarian. For economic and often religious reasons, the majority of the world eats beans! In the U.S., about one in fifty people is now at least a partial vegetarian (one who eats no red meat, and sometimes no seafood or poultry either).

Beans are one of the most inexpensive sources of protein available. You can create a bean meal of chili, soup, stew or casserole for less than fifty cents a serving.

Many people avoid beans because 1) they think beans are hard to cook, 2) they don't know how to prepare them properly and make them taste good, or 3) they are concerned about gas.

Let's try to put some of these common fears to rest. Beans (or legumes) include peas and lentils too. They can be bought canned or dried. Although dried beans are more nutritious, it is better to use canned beans when in a hurry rather than eat none at all. Just open the can and rinse the beans thoroughly to remove any juices which may cause gas. I prefer to cook *all* canned beans either by heating in a saucepan or steaming to further reduce gas, remove any possible additives and make them more digestible. If you are adding them to a salad, heat them and quick-chill them in the freezer before using.

If you are cooking dried beans, follow the directions below. Although it may seem like a long process to prepare dried beans, it is actually very simple. It takes time to soak and cook the beans, but they need little tending during either process. I have often left the house to go shopping and left the beans cooking on low heat on the stove or in a slow cooker or crock pot. It is just as easy to make a large batch of beans as a small one, so make two, three or four times a recipe and freeze the leftovers. Beans will keep refrigerated for 7–8 days or frozen for up to 3 months and are one of the few foods that can be re-frozen.

One of the biggest fears people have about eating beans is getting gas. It does take a little time to get used to digesting beans. Note the tips below for extra help. At most health food stores, pharmacies and some markets there are also excellent products available with helpful enzymes which naturally assist your body in digesting beans without worry about embarrassing flatulence.

Once you have included beans in your diet, you'll wonder how you ever did without them! They are hearty and satisfying and many of my cooking students have remarked that they "feel wonderful the next day after eating them." It makes them "feel grounded." Also some vegetarians who find themselves getting cold in winter will find that beans "warm their insides" and they'll feel "warm through and through" from eating them.

As Thoreau wrote in *Walden*, "I grew to love my rows, my beans. They attached me to the earth like Antaeus. I got strength from them." (In Greek mythology, Antaeus was a warrior who was undefeatable as long as his feet were touching the earth.)

Personally, beans are one of my favourite foods and I consider them a vital source of my energy, power and stamina. To know beans is to love them! But don't take my word for it, try them for yourself. Then you can "toot" your own horn in praise of beans!

How to Cook Beans Properly for Good Digestion (And No Gas!)

1. Measure the amount of beans (peas/legumes) required and sort through them and remove any misshapen, discoloured or damaged beans. Also remove any dirt balls, gravel or other foreign objects and discard them.

2. Soak 1 cup of dry beans in 3–4 cups of cool or room temperature water and let the beans soak 8 hours or more uncovered. Soak chick peas 12 hours or more and soak soybeans 24 hours. Avoid using soybeans as they usually require a pressure cooker.

3. *Important:* Throw away the water the beans soaked in. This soaking water contains a gas released by the beans while soaking, which in turn will give you gas.

4. Rinse the beans several times and swish them around in fresh water.

5. Put the beans in a large pot so that beans fill only about half of the pot and add fresh water until the beans are covered by 1" or so of water.

6. Bring the beans and water, uncovered, to a boil on high heat.

7. When the beans are boiling, a white foam or froth will generally form on top. Scoop this off and discard it. This is part of what contributes to gas.

8. Add extra water if needed so the beans are still at least 1" under water. Turn the heat down to very low, just low enough so the beans are barely bubbling, and cover them. They cook fastest at this temperature and retain more nutrients. Cook for 1¼–3 hours until tender. (Most beans cook in 2 hours or less. Chick peas and soybeans may require 2–3 hours.)

9. *Optional:* Add 1 tsp. ground fennel or preferably 1 tsp. savoury to the beans while cooking. This improves their digestibility. Cooking beans with sea kelp or seaweeds also helps to eliminate gas, but these must be added after the beans are already tender.

10. Cook for 1¼ hours or more until the beans are very tender and a bean can easily be mashed with the tongue on the roof of the mouth.

11. Always chew beans slowly, never eat them fast or when under excessive stress or fatigue.

12. Have some raw foods or salad first in a meal before eating the beans, to aid in their digestion.

13. Make sure not to add any oil, salt or salty ingredients like seaweed to beans while they are cooking. These ingredients can actually toughen the beans so they stay hard. When they are completely tender in the cooking pot, then add these ingredients. Added after the beans are soft, oil and salt actually *help* them to become more digestible.

14. For those with excessive gas problems, bring dry beans to

a boil in their soaking water, then let them cool down, uncovered, for 6–8 hours (8–12 hours for chick peas; 12–24 hours for soybeans) before changing the water and cooking. (In hot weather, beans must be refrigerated after the first few hours.) Another help for extreme cases is to sprout the beans before cooking, but this may alter the taste somewhat.

15. The easiest-to-digest beans are lentils, adzuki beans, pinto beans and chick peas. Those with sensitive digestion should try these first. People over age 60 who are not accustomed to beans should avoid all except the lentils and very occasionally cooked, mashed beans with other foods.

16. 1 cup dry beans makes about 2½ cups soaked or cooked beans.

Beverages

This book includes brief information on water, juices and herb teas, and a chapter on substitute milk beverages. Mixed fruit drinks and punches are popular drinks easy to create by mixing a few fruits and/or juices together with optional sweetener, mineral water, etc. For a wide assortment of recipes for these beverages, see *The All Natural Allergy Cookbook* or *For the Love of Food.*

WATER

Water is the most important of all beverages. For optimum health, drink 3–6 glasses daily. Drink it slowly, upon rising and throughout the day, but not with meals. Tested spring water and water purified by reverse osmosis are the best drinking waters for most people. Distilled water is good only when the daily diet includes plenty of vitamin- and mineral rich foods or supplements. Distilled water should be used for fasting, cleansing and healing diets.

How to Make Herb Teas

Leaf or Flower Tea (and powdered rose hips): Use one teaspoon of loose tea per cup. Steep only. Boiling makes the tea bitter and also kills valuable vitamins and enzymes. To steep, boil the water. When it comes to a bubbling boil, remove the water from the heat, put it into a teapot, add the tea and cover the pot.

Let it steep (sit) for 8–12 minutes, then strain and drink. A tea ball may be used for leaf and flower teas *only*.

Seed or Twig Teas (and crushed and broken rose hips): Use ¼–½ teaspoon of loose tea per cup. Bring water and tea to a boil together and let it simmer on just a low bubble for 5–10 minutes. Then let it steep for another 10 minutes off the heat. Strain and drink.

Root or Bark Tea (and whole rose hips): Use ¼–½ teaspoon root or bark, broken or chopped into small pieces, per cup. Make sure tea is broken up as much as possible. Prepare the same as seed and twig tea except simmer it on a low bubble for 15–20 minutes instead of 5–10. Follow with steeping for 10 minutes. Strain and drink.

Powdered Root or Powdered Bark Tea: Use ¹⁄₁₀–¹⁄₁₆ teaspoon powdered tea per cup. Mix the tea and water well before heating. Then bring to a boil and simmer on a low bubble for 20–30 minutes. Let sit a few minutes before drinking.

All Herb Teabags: Each herb teabag can be used to make 2–3 cups of herb tea. For the first cup of tea, *add* the teabag to the hot water so the flavour will not be too strong or too bitter. For more cups from the same bag, pour hot water over the teabag for full flavour. If the teabag is fragile, don't pour the hot water directly onto the bag but rather off to the side so the bag does not break and spoil the tea. If the bag should break, strain the tea with a small bamboo or stainless steel strainer. For teapots, add one teabag for each 2 cups water. Add the bag to the water and cover the pot while the tea steeps.

How to Make Herb Tea Combinations: When making an herb tea combination, special care must be taken not to overcook the teas. For example, when making a combination of twig and leaf tea, one cannot boil the leaf tea with the twig tea or the tea would become bitter and lose nutrients. Leaf tea should never be boiled! The twig tea should be low boiled *by itself* and the leaf tea should be added to the boiled twig tea during the steeping time only. For orange and lemon peels, use only unsprayed, organic fruit rinds and prepare like twig tea. Stir teas with cinnamon sticks for added flavour.

Some Herb Tea Combinations
1. Peppermint, alfalfa, chamomile
2. Spearmint and strawberry leaves
3. Peppermint, alfalfa, comfrey, lemon grass
4. Raspberry leaves and comfrey poured over lemon slices
5. Rose hips, strawberry or raspberry leaves and orange rind
6. Fennel seeds and alfalfa leaves
7. Fenugreek seeds and mint leaves
8. Rose hips, peppermint and slippery elm powder
9. Create your own combinations!

Caution: Stick with the bulk (loose) teas mentioned here and flower teas like lavender and hibiscus for pleasure drinking. Some bulk teas have strong medicinal powers and can cause stomach upset, headaches or nausea if used incorrectly. Consult your health food store for more information.

DAIRY-FREE "MILKS"

Cashew Nut Milk

1 cup water

2–3 Tbsp. ground or whole raw cashew pieces

Blend ingredients thoroughly in a blender for several minutes until the water becomes white. Strain if necessary and stir well before using. Keeps 1–3 days in the refrigerator, or may be frozen for later use.

Note: Technically speaking, all cashews must be slightly cooked before being sold. Buy the ones called "raw" in the store.

Thick Cashew Nut Milk

Follow the directions for **Cashew Nut Milk** (above), but use 3–4 Tbsp. cashews instead of 2–3.

Sweet Cashew Nut Milk

1 cup water
2–4 Tbsp. ground or whole raw cashew pieces
1–3 Tbsp. sweetener *or* 2–4 pitted dates
Dash or two of sea salt

Optional: ½ tsp. real vanilla flavouring or other flavouring
Optional: 1–2 tsp. natural light oil

Follow the directions for **Cashew Nut Milk** (above).

Blanched Almond Nut Milk

Follow the directions for any of the three **Cashew Nut Milks** (above), but use blanched almonds instead of cashew pieces.

Sesame or Sunflower Seed Milk

1 cup water
⅓ cup raw sesame seeds,
   hulled or unhulled, *or*
   ⅓–½ cup hulled
   sunflower seeds

Optional: 1–3 Tbsp.
   sweetener *or* 2–3 pitted
   dates

It is best to grind the seeds in the blender first, grinding half of the required amount at a time. Then blend all the ingredients thoroughly and strain twice through a fine strainer or cheesecloth. Some sweeteners may be added after straining, if desired. Do not use sweetener if milk is to be used in non-dessert or beverage recipes. Keeps several days refrigerated.

Soy Milk

2 cups water
2–4 Tbsp. instant soy milk
   powder
Optional: ½ tsp. real vanilla
   flavouring*

Optional: 1–3 Tbsp.
   sweetener *or* 2–4 pitted
   dates

Blend ingredients well and stir before each use. Strain if dates are used. Keeps a few days refrigerated.

   *Add a few drops of maple, butterscotch, nut or mint flavouring with or instead of the vanilla, if desired.

Coconut Milk

1 cup water   ¼–½ cup shredded
                                 unsweetened coconut

Blend ingredients thoroughly and strain if needed. Coconut milk
adds a coconut flavour to recipes. Add extra sweetening if desired.
Great for use in Oriental recipes, some sauces and desserts. A nice
occasional milk, as it is somewhat high in fat and calories
compared to other milks.

Alfalfa Milk

1 cup alfalfa sprouts   Water

Rinse the sprouts thoroughly to remove all brown hulls, or cut off
the brown seed hulls if necessary. Blend the sprouts in the blender
with just enough water to keep the blades turning well, and create
a "milk". Add extra water if necessary to create the desired
consistency. Straining is optional. Use with or without sweeteners
in recipes.

Zucchini Milk

1 cup grated zucchini   Water

Choose firm, fresh, bright green and white coloured zucchini. The
dark or yellowish ones are bitter. Peel zucchini if desired. Blend
the grated zucchini in the blender with just enough water to keep
the blades turning well and create a thick, white "milk." Add extra
water or strain if desired. Use with or without sweetening in
recipes.

Carob Milk

2 cups thick cashew, almond
  or soy milk
2–4 Tbsp. sweetener *or* 4–8
  pitted dates

½ tsp. real vanilla flavouring
⅛ tsp. maple, nut, mint,
  rum or other flavouring
5–8 tsp. carob powder

Blend ingredients well and serve stirred and chilled. Use within 1–3 days and keep refrigerated.

For **Hot Carob Milk**, follow the directions above. Heat on medium heat, then simmer, stirring, 1 minute or until hot. Serve immediately with a cinnamon stick or a sprinkle of cinnamon. Delicious!

Carob Malted

Follow the directions for **Carob Milk** (above), using 7–8 tsp. carob powder. Add 3 Tbsp. barley malt powder or syrup, and add another sweetener if desired. Optional flavour enhancers are 1 tsp. natural light oil and a few dashes of sea salt. Blend very well, chill and serve. Use within 1–2 days. Keep refrigerated.

Carob Shake

Follow the directions for **Carob Milk** (above), but add 1 whole banana and/or 1 scoop of natural vegan vanilla ice cream.

Other Milk Substitutes

Soy milks, rice milks, coconut and other liquid and powdered milks can be purchased in your health food store and some supermarkets. Use these in recipes from this book or in place of dairy milk in other cookbooks. There will be some change in flavour.

Breakfasts

PREPARING CEREAL GRAINS

Be sure to read "Special Tips on Whole Grains," in the chapter on Special Foods.

Raw Cereals

Flaked whole-grain cereals such as flaked oats, rye, wheat, rice, barley and millet are not always available. Prepare and serve them like soaked organic rolled oats (below), or toast them in the oven like granola and serve with milk substitute and flavourings.

Granola and other toasted grain cereals are made with toasted rolled oats or other rolled grain, nuts and seeds, dried fruit, sweetening, etc. Serve with milk substitute or fruit juice, or eat them right out of the package. Chew them well.

Muesli and other raw cereals are usually made with rolled, cracked or flaked whole grains, ground or chopped nuts and seeds, and sometimes shredded coconut, raisins or other dried fruits. If the cereal is organic or contains very tough, fibrous grains, prepare it the same way as soaked organic rolled oats (below). If the cereal is just natural and less fibrous, prepare it the same way as soaked natural rolled oats (below).

Natural rolled oats (regular or old-fashioned) Soak 1 cup oats in 1 cup of very warm water for 10–15 minutes. Add flavourings and/or cut fruit, and serve.

Organic rolled oats are smaller and rounder than natural rolled oats and must be soaked for several hours or overnight before eating, unless they are "crushed" or chopped after rolling, then they soak or cook as easily as natural oats. These are usually found only in health food stores and are almost always labelled "organic." After soaking in 1–1½ cups very warm water per 1 cup of oats, drain off excess water (if any) and serve with sweetening, milk substitute and/or fruit.

Rolled rice, rye, wheat or barley can be used in place of oats in recipes, if available.

Puffed whole-grain cereals include puffed amaranth, oats, corn, rice, millet, wheat and others. They are usually unsweetened. Serve them as they are with milk substitute and sweetening as desired.

Cooked Cereals

Amaranth. Although amaranth grain can be cooked as a breakfast cereal, it is not that tasty. It is better to use the flour in recipes or buy the puffed amaranth cereal available in many health food stores. Notice that it is usually added to a cereal rather than sold by itself as a cereal. If desired, cook it in 2 times as much water for a rice like texture, and 2½–3 times as much water for cereal or to add to breads. Cook until tender, about 18–20 minutes.

Cornmeal. Use 2–2½ cups water per 1 cup cornmeal. The coarser the meal, the more water is needed and the longer the cooking time. Start water and cornmeal cooking together in cool or lukewarm water and stir together on medium heat. Use a wire whisk to make sure the cereal does not become lumpy. After 1–2 minutes, the cereal must be stirred constantly for 10 minutes or more until it is no longer grainy. Add extra water if needed. Cornmeal should always have a sweetener like maple syrup added to it. Raisins, dates, or coconut and cinnamon cooked into the cereal are also very delicious. Sea salt is optional. Store dry cornmeal in a cool place or in the freezer, but never refrigerate it or it will have a damp, musty flavour.

Quinoa (pronounced *keen-wah*). Rinse thoroughly before cooking by rubbing the grains together well in a pot of water and changing the water 2–4 times. This helps to remove the saponin, which may irritate digestion or allergies. Cook like millet (see below), but use 2–3 cups water to 1 cup quinoa and cook 20–30 minutes until tender.

Millet (cereal). Use 3–4 cups of water per 1 cup millet. (More water is used for the cereal than for main dish millet.) Bring water and millet to a boil. Dates can be added now if desired—delicious! Use ¼–½ cup dates per 1 cup millet. Then turn down heat and simmer, covered, for 50–60 minutes until the millet breaks down and is very soft and mushy. Before serving, stir the cereal to mix in the dates. Serve with milk substitute or juice and oil and also maple syrup or other sweetener, if no dates are added. Add sea salt if desired.

Cooked oatmeal. *Whole rolled natural oatmeal and chopped rolled organic oatmeal* (regular or old-fashioned): Use 1–1½ cups water per 1 cup natural rolled oats. Bring water to a boil and add oats. Stir once, cover and remove from heat. Let sit for 10–15 minutes before serving. Add flavourings to taste. Another method for these types of oats is the soaked oats method: Put the oats in a sturdy bowl and pour very hot or boiling water over them. Cover and let sit 10–15 minutes. Do not stir! Add flavourings or stewed or fresh fruit and enjoy. This method preserves more of the beneficial enzymes found in oats, and many people feel the oats taste better because they do not get gummy or sticky. *Whole rolled organic oatmeal:* Use 1½–2 cups water per 1 cup organic rolled oats. Bring the water to a boil, then turn down heat and add oats. Stir constantly and cook for 5–10 minutes or until oats are easy to chew. Then turn off heat, cover oatmeal and let it sit for 10–15 minutes before serving. Add flavourings to taste.

Whole oats, whole triticale, whole wheat kernels (wheat

berries—hard red or soft yellow) and **whole spelt**. Cook as for main dish oats. Serve plain with sea salt, with oil and maple syrup.

Sweet brown rice. Cook and serve like millet cereal (above), but use 2–3 cups water per 1 cup rice and cook it for 50–60 minutes until tender.

Teff. Bring ½ cup teff seed and 2 cups of water to a boil, then turn down heat and simmer for 15–20 minutes or until all the water is absorbed. Cook ¼ cup raisins, currants or dates with the teff if desired. If dried fruit is not used, serve the cereal with maple syrup, fruit concentrate or other sweetener and a bit of sea salt or cinnamon.

Rice-Ola (Rice Granola)
(Serves 6 or more)

2 cups cold, cooked brown rice

2 cups rice bran (stabilized is best)

1 cup ground nuts *or* sunflower seeds

½ cup maple syrup *or* fruit concentrate

⅓ cup natural light oil

¾ tsp. sea salt

Optional: 1 tsp. cinnamon or allspice *or* 2 Tbsp. carob powder

Optional: ½–1 cup dried fruit

Preheat the oven to 350°F. Mix all the ingredients together carefully with a fork. Spread the mixture evenly on a lightly oiled, large, flat baking pan. Bake for about 25 minutes, stirring or turning the mixture completely every 8–10 minutes until lightly browned. Add dried fruit and allow the mixture to cool and harden 1 hour before storing. Store in a sealed container for up to 3 weeks at room temperature, or refrigerate. Do not overbake!

Granola
(Serves 2 or more)

6–8 cups rolled oats
4–6 cups mixed chopped
    nuts, seeds and dried fruit
½–⅔ cup natural light oil

1–1½ cups maple syrup *or*
    other liquid sweetener
1 tsp. sea salt

Mix together the oats, nuts and seeds, but set aside the dried fruit. In a separate bowl combine the oil, sweetener and salt and mix well. Add the dry mixture to the wet and mix together with a large wooden spoon or with your hands. Preheat the oven to 350°F. Lightly oil two flat baking pans or pizza pans and spread the granola mixture on them about ½–⅔" deep. Bake for 12–18 minutes until the top layer is browned. Then remove the granola from the oven, stir or turn all the granola and replace it in the oven. Bake it for another 4–5 minutes and remove and stir again. Add the dried fruit. Bake the granola for a final 4–5 minutes and remove it from the oven into a large bowl. The mixture will be moist, but it will become crisp and hard as it cools.

Let the granola cool before storing. Break it up every 10 minutes or so as it cools to keep it from hardening into one lump. When cool, store covered in the refrigerator or in a jar or tin in a cool, dry place. Enjoy dry if chewed well, or serve with fruit juice (apple, peach or pear are best), a milk substitute, applesauce or cooked fruit syrup. Also sprinkle it over ice cream, cakes or other desserts. Add a few tablespoons of flax seeds to the granola before baking for added nutrients or add ½–1 tsp. ground raw flax seed to the cereal before eating.

Millet-Fruit Squares
(Makes 9–16 squares)

Crust:
1½ cups millet (wash first)
3¾ cups water
¼ cup maple syrup *or* other
   liquid sweetener
Optional: ¼–½ tsp. sea salt

¾–1 cup ground raw nuts or
   seeds

Fruit Filling:
1½ cups dried apricots,
   dates, figs, raisins or other
   fruit, chopped
4 dried pineapple rings,
   chopped *or* another ½
   cup other dried fruit,
   chopped
3–4 tsp. grated lemon or
   orange rind
4–5 Tbsp. lemon, orange or
   pineapple juice
¾ cup water

Cook the millet in the water for about 45 minutes and cool. Preheat the oven to 350°F. Gently stir the sweetener and salt into the millet, and spread half the mixture in an oiled 9"x9" square baking pan. Sprinkle ¼–½ cup of nuts over it and bake about 10 minutes. Let cool.

While the millet is cooking, combine the fruit filling ingredients in a saucepan, bring to a low boil, then simmer on low to medium low heat for 30–45 minutes or until the fruit can be stirred easily into a mushy fruit spread. Allow to cool completely.

Use most or all of the fruit mixture (depending on how sweet you would like the squares to be), and spread it over the first layer of baked millet. Sprinkle on more ground nuts if desired. Add the last of the cooled millet mixture and spread it evenly over the fruit. Add additional ground nuts or seeds if desired. Bake for about 20 minutes more at 350°F until somewhat dryer and firm. Cool completely and chill to help set the squares. Serve at room temperature. Keeps 6–8 days refrigerated. Great for lunches and snacks too. Some prefer this as a dessert, as is, or with ¼ cup or more powdered natural sweetener added to the millet.

Easy Millet-Fruit Parfaits
(Makes 8–14)

Prepare the hot millet and fruit filling as in the **Millet-Fruit Squares** (above). Optional dry cereal or granola may also be added. Layer a parfait glass with the millet mixture, then ground nuts or seeds, fruit filling, then additional dry cereal if desired. Repeat the layering and top with nuts, raisins or coconut. Chill and serve for breakfast or dessert. If a sweeter dessert is desired, add extra powdered natural sweetener to the millet mixture.

Scrambled Tofu
(Serves 2–3)

2 Tbsp. natural oil
2–3 green onions, diced
½ cup finely chopped green
   pepper
7–9 mushrooms, chopped
14–16 oz (400–450 g)
   regular tofu, crumbled
2–3 tsp. tamari soy sauce
½ tsp. sea salt
½ tsp. curry powder
Several dashes cayenne
   pepper
Optional: several dashes
   turmeric (for a yellow
   colour)

In a frying pan, heat the oil and sauté the onions, pepper and mushrooms for about 2 minutes. Add the tofu and remaining ingredients and sauté for 3–6 minutes more, until the flavours mingle and the mixture is hot throughout. Serve immediately with toast, vegetable sticks, a salad, tomato slices, artichoke hearts or your favourite accompaniment.

Brown Rice Breakfast Chews

1 cup cooked brown rice
2 Tbsp. maple syrup *or* fruit
   concentrate
¼–½ cup whole or chopped
   almonds or other nuts

¼–½ cup raisins *or* currants*
¼ cup tapioca flour
2 Tbsp. arrowroot powder
1 tsp. cinnamon
Several dashes sea salt

To prepare the 1 cup brown rice, use about ½ cup uncooked rice. Be sure to measure after cooking, however, as some rice varieties expand more.

Preheat the oven to 300°F. With a fork, mix the cooked rice with the other ingredients, being careful not to mash or crush the rice. When all the flour and arrowroot powder are fully mixed in, drop by heaping teaspoonfuls onto lightly oiled cookie sheets, 1½–2 inches apart. Flatten each ball to a thickness of ⅜"–½" and bake for 40–50 minutes until firm and lightly browned. Cool for 1 hour and then store in a tin for 1–2 days at room temperature, or 3–7 days in the refrigerator.

*Instead of raisins or currants, you may use chopped dates, dried apricots, dried apples, or extra seeds or chopped nuts. A simple, satisfying snack for breakfasts on the run or afternoon nibbles. Makes 18–20 chews.

Whole Grain Pancakes
(Serves 2)

Wet ingredients:
¾–⅞ cup apple, peach or
 pear juice
4 tsp. natural light oil

Dry ingredients:
½ cup flour: whole wheat,
 kamut, spelt, quinoa,
 millet, teff, amaranth or
 buckwheat

½ cup light flour: whole
 wheat pastry, unbleached
 white, tapioca or brown
 rice
⅓ cup arrowroot powder
4 tsp. baking powder
¼ tsp. sea salt

Mix the wet ingredients together. In a separate bowl, mix the dry ingredients together. Avoid using cinnamon in this recipe as it may hinder rising.

Oil a frying pan and bring it quickly to medium-high heat. Add the dry ingredients to the wet and mix well, adding enough juice to thin it to the desired consistency. Start making the pancakes immediately after the batter is mixed. Cook for about 1 minute until the edges dry up a bit. (Watch the heat or the pancakes will cook too fast and burn.) Turn over and cook another 15–30 seconds. Do not flatten the pancakes when turning them! Turn again to check for doneness, then flatten if desired. Re-oil the frying pan generously before starting each new batch. Enjoy these pancakes with maple syrup, jam, mixed chopped fruit, **Strawberry Special Topping** or **Fruit Delight Topping**.

Tofu French Toast
(Serves 2–4)

Dipping Mixture:
7–8 oz (250 g) regular tofu, crumbled
¾ cup **Soy Milk, Nut Milk, Coconut Milk** or water
1–2 Tbsp. natural light oil
3–4 tsp. liquid sweetener
1 tsp. real vanilla
½ tsp. cinnamon
Several dashes sea salt

Bread

Maple syrup *or* other liquid sweetener
Stewed fruit or jam
Chopped nuts and/or seeds
Shredded unsweetened coconut

Blend all Dipping Mixture ingredients together in a blender or food processor. Heat a well-oiled frying pan on medium-high heat. Dip the bread in the tofu mixture and place several slices in the hot pan. Cook a few minutes on each side until lightly browned. Make sure to re-oil the pan before cooking each batch. Serve with toppings and coconut if desired.

Special Breakfast Ideas

1. Half a **Baked Butternut** or **Buttercup Squash** sprinkled with cinnamon and ¼–½ cup **Home Roasted Nuts**.

2. **Orange Yam Sauce** on toast or on **Easy Tamari Tofu Sauté**.

3. Breakfast whole grains served with **Vegetarian Gravy, Mushroom Gravy, Avocado Tofu Sauce, Creamy Cashew Sauce, Toasted Sesame Sauce** or **Toasted Cashew Sauce**.

4. Steamed cauliflower with **Tomato Sauce** or **Mock Tomato Sauce** and raw grated or ribboned zucchini.

5. **Tofu Rarebit, Grilled Tofu, Rice and Raisin Pudding, Wonderful Millet Vegetable Balls** and various "burger" recipes make terrific alternate breakfasts. Use your imagination to transform other main dish foods into hearty breakfast ideas.

Snacks, Spreads, Dips

Royal Snack Mix

1 cup raw sunflower seeds
1 cup raisins *or* currants
¼ cup raw cashew pieces
¼ cup raw almonds

Optional: ½ cup shredded or
ribbon unsweetened
coconut

Mix all ingredients together and store in tins, jars or plastic bags for freshness. Keeps several weeks or longer.

Garden Snack Mix

1 cup raw hulled pumpkin
seeds (pepitas)
1 cup pecans *or* fresh walnuts
½ cup dried apricots

½ cup pine nuts *or*
hazelnuts (filberts)
½ cup other dried fruit
(pears, peaches, apples,
etc.)

Mix all ingredients together and store in tins, jars or plastic bags for freshness. Keeps several weeks or longer.

Olive and Nut Dip

7–8 oz (250 g) regular tofu
½ cup green olives with
  pimento *or* black olives
⅓ cup **Home Roasted Nuts:**
  almonds, cashews, Brazils,
  hazelnuts (filberts) or
  pecans

3–4 Tbsp. lemon juice
1–2 Tbsp. chopped green
  onion tops *or* chives
1 Tbsp. natural oil
¼ tsp. sea salt

Combine everything in a food processor until smooth. Chill and serve. Keeps 3–6 days refrigerated.

Spinach Tofu Dip

1 lb spinach (2 cups firmly
  packed)
6–8 oz (250 g) tofu,
  crumbled
2–3 tsp. parsley
1–2 tsp. tamari soy sauce *or*
  miso
½ tsp. basil

¼ tsp. *each* paprika and
  oregano
⅛ tsp. *each* marjoram and
  thyme
Several dashes *each* cayenne
  pepper and sea kelp
Optional: ½ cup **Home
  Roasted Nuts**

Steam the spinach 8–12 minutes until tender. Wash the tofu and dry off excess water. Liquefy all ingredients in a food processor, or use a blender, adding a few drops of water if necessary and stopping occasionally to stir the dip. Correct seasonings to taste. Serve the dip in hollowed-out vegetables or bread and dip crackers or fresh vegetables in it, or spread it on bread. Keeps 3–6 days refrigerated.

Carrot Tofu Dip

Follow the directions for **Spinach Tofu Dip** (above), but use 3–4 medium carrots instead of the spinach. Also add 1 tsp. dill weed to the dip.

Tofu Mock Egg Salad

12–14 oz (350–400 g) tofu, crumbled

2 stalks celery *or* ½ green pepper, very finely chopped

1 medium tomato, seeded, very finely chopped and towel dried

5–7 green onion tops, finely chopped

½ tsp. garlic powder

¼ tsp. paprika

Vegetable sea salt to taste

Several dashes *each* cayenne pepper and sea kelp

Optional: several dashes turmeric, for a yellow colour

Optional: ¼ tsp. celery seed

Optional: 1 tsp. parsley

Combine all ingredients in a bowl with a spoon. Mix well, but gently. Serve with crackers or in pita bread wedges. It can also be stuffed into tomatoes, bell peppers or celery. Keeps 2–4 days refrigerated.

Guacamole

1 large ripe avocado, peeled, pitted and mashed

1 small tomato, seeded and diced

1 tsp. minced onion *or* onion powder

¼–½ tsp. chili powder

Vegetable sea salt to taste

3–5 tsp. fresh lemon juice (essential to keep the avocado from turning brown)

Few dashes sea kelp

Optional: few drops tamari soy sauce

Optional: 8–14 chopped black olives

Mix all the ingredients together and chill before using as a dip or spread, or as a topping or side dish with Mexican food. If it is used as a dip, bury the avocado pit in the bottom of the dip bowl. This will keep the dip fresh longer.

8-Layer Mexican Dip

1. **Bravo Burrito** beans (½–1 batch)
2. Salsa (½–1 cup)
3. Chopped lettuce (2–3 cups)
4. Chopped tomatoes (2–3 cups)
5. Chopped green peppers (2–3 cups)
6. Dairy- and casein-free soy cheese, brick, cheddar or mozzarella style, grated; or **Easy Tamari Tofu Sauté** (1 batch), in chunks
7. Guacamole (2–3 batches)
8. Black olives (½ cup or more, sliced)

Choose a deep, 1½–2 quart glass bowl of uniform depth. Arrange the ingredients in layers, beginning with the beans, so that the layers are visible through the glass. Serve with corn chips and flour tortilla wedges for a special party treat, snack or meal.

Tofu Curry Dip

7–8 oz (250 g) regular tofu
¾ cup **Nut Milk** or **Soy Milk**
2 Tbsp. raw ground cashew pieces or blanched almonds
1 Tbsp. arrowroot powder or 1 tsp. guar gum or xanthan gum
2–3 tsp. liquid sweetener

1–1¼ tsp. curry powder
½ tsp. turmeric
¼ tsp. *each* paprika, cumin and chili powder
⅛ tsp. ginger
Sea salt *or* vegetable sea salt to taste
Cayenne pepper to taste

Combine all ingredients in a blender or food processor. Chill 1 hour before serving as a dressing or vegetable dip. Keeps 5–7 days in the refrigerator.

Middle Eastern Falafel Spread

1 cup dry chick peas
½ cup sesame tahini
1–2 cloves garlic, minced
1–2 tsp. grated or very finely
    chopped onion
2–4 tsp. tamari soy sauce
2 tsp. parsley

1 tsp. cumin seeds or
    powder (cominos)
1 tsp. chili powder
½–1 tsp. sea salt
¼ tsp. celery seed
¼ tsp. sea kelp
Several dashes cayenne
    pepper, to taste

Soak the chick peas and cook until very tender, then drain and save the liquid. While the chick peas are still very hot, mash them with the remaining ingredients. Add ½–1 cup of the reserved cooking liquid as needed to make a spreading consistency, and adjust herbs and spices to taste.

You may use a bit less liquid in the spread and add a bit of flour, roll the falafel into balls and pan-fry them, or shape them into patties and pan-grill them. Traditionally, falafel balls were deep-fried, but this is an unnecessary addition of fats to the diet.

Leftover spread can be refrigerated for up to 7–8 days, or stored in the freezer for up to 3 months. Make double and triple batches and freeze extras for quick high-protein/calcium meals and snacks. Delicious stuffed in celery sticks or partially hollowed-out tomatoes.

Humus (Hummous) Spread
(Serves 6–8)

1 cup dry chick peas
   (garbanzos), soaked,
   cooked and drained
½ cup sesame tahini
1–2 cups bean cooking liquid
⅓–½ cup fresh lemon juice
1 small onion, chopped
3–6 cloves garlic, pressed

2 Tbsp. tamari soy sauce
¾–1 tsp. sea salt *or* vegetable
   sea salt, to taste
1 tsp. paprika
⅛ tsp. sea kelp
Cayenne pepper to taste
Optional: 1–2 tsp. olive oil

Cook the chick peas until they are tender enough to mash with your tongue on the roof of your mouth. Drain and save the bean cooking liquid. Hand mash or use a food processor to combine the chick peas and tahini. Mash thoroughly. Blend the bean liquid, lemon juice and tamari with the onion, garlic and herbs for the best results. (These can also be added to the food processor, or just dice the onion and garlic very small.) Mash or mix all the ingredients together and serve warm or chilled with pita breads or crackers, stuffed into celery or used as a dip or spread. Keeps 7–8 days refrigerated and is great for freezing. Make double and triple batches. Great meal or snacking food!

Easy Sunflower Pâté*
(Serves 6–8)

Dry ingredients:

1 cup sunflower seeds, finely ground

½ cup cornmeal, kamut flour *or* amaranth flour

½ cup engevita or other yellow nutritional yeast, powdered

3 tsp. dried parsley flakes, crushed

1½ tsp. dried basil, crushed

1 tsp. dried thyme, crushed

¾–1 tsp. sea salt

½ tsp. dried sage leaves, finely crushed

¼ tsp. sea kelp

1 cup finely grated potato

1⅓ cups water

¼ cup sunflower oil or other natural oil

2 Tbsp. tamari soy sauce

3–4 tsp. prepared horseradish

Mix the dry ingredients together in a bowl. Grate the potato and rinse it thoroughly to remove excess starch. Squeeze and drain it after rinsing. Add the remaining ingredients in the order given, stirring in the potato last. Mix well.

Preheat the oven to 375°F. Generously oil a 9" glass pie plate and scoop in the pâté mixture. Put it in the oven and immediately turn the heat down to 350°F. Bake 35–45 minutes until well browned.

Let the pâté cool 1–2 hours and then chill it thoroughly before serving to set it completely. It may be reheated later if desired. It is tastiest when served at room temperature. Enjoy the pâté as an appetizer, snack or protein main dish. May be served with crackers or bread. Great for picnics, lunches or parties. Keeps up to 7 days refrigerated, or may be frozen in pie wedges.

*With reduced oil and no onions or garlic.

Hazelnut Pâté
(Serves 6–8)

Dry ingredients:
1½ cups hazelnut flour *or* raw, finely ground hazelnuts (filberts)
½ cup kamut or spelt flour*
3 tsp. dried parsley flakes, crushed
1½ tsp. dried basil, crushed
1 tsp. sea salt
1 tsp. ground mustard
1 tsp. thyme, crushed
½ tsp. sage, well crushed
¼ tsp. sea kelp (important to flavour)
Several dashes cayenne pepper

Wet ingredients:
2 cups water
⅓ cup natural oil
3 Tbsp. tamari soy sauce *or* 2 vegetable bouillon cubes with 4 Tbsp. water
4 tsp. prepared horseradish
1 Tbsp. toasted sesame oil

1 cup finely grated carrot
Optional: ¼–½ cup finely chopped, sautéed mushrooms

Preheat the oven to 350°F. Mix all the dry ingredients together in a bowl. Mix all the wet ingredients with the carrot. (If bouillon cubes are used, mash or blend them with the water first.) Lightly oil a 9" glass pie plate and scoop in the pâté mixture. Bake about 35–40 minutes until set and browned. Let cool 1–2 hours and then chill thoroughly to set it completely before serving. It is tastiest when served at room temperature. Enjoy the pâté as an appetizer, snack or protein main dish. May be served alone or with crackers or bread. Great for picnics, lunches or parties. Keeps up to 7 days refrigerated, or may be frozen in pie wedges.

*Oat flour, quinoa flour or millet flour may be substituted for the kamut or spelt if necessary, with altered flavour. Add 1 Tbsp. arrowroot with other flours to total ½ cup. Yeast-free!

Salads

Early Garden Salad
(Serves 2–4)

8–12 leaves leaf lettuce, torn
8–12 leaves sorrel or
   spinach, torn
3–6 baby carrots, grated

1–2 new potatoes, small
   turnips *or* parsnips, grated
6–10 radishes, sliced thin
Optional: 1–3 green onions,
   tops only, chopped

Wash and prepare all the vegetables just before mealtime. Toss gently in the **Herbs and Oil Dressing** or **Lemon Herb Dressing** and serve.

Romaine Salad
(Serves 2)

6–10 leaves romaine lettuce,
   torn
2 stalks celery, sliced thin
1 small turnip, parsnip *or*
   new potato, grated very
   fine

½–¾ cup red cabbage,
   shredded very fine, *or* 1
   red bell pepper, cut in
   thin strips
Optional: chopped green
   onions *or* chives

Mix all ingredients together. Toss and serve with a favourite dressing.

Classic Green Salad
(Serves 2–4)

4–6 leaves romaine, red or
  leaf lettuce
½ bunch spinach, leaves only
½ head Boston or bibb
  lettuce
1–2 tomatoes, cut in thin
  wedges

¼–½ cucumber or English
  cucumber, sliced in
  rounds or quarter rounds
½–1 green, red, purple or
  yellow bell pepper, cut in
  strips

Wash and tear the greens into bite-sized pieces. Toss everything together and serve with an oil or creamy dressing.

Spinach Salad
(Serves 2–4)

1 small bunch of spinach,
  leaves only, stems
  removed
1 small zucchini, sliced in
  rounds or half rounds

1 large carrot *or* medium
  beet, grated
a large avocado, cut in
  chunks, *or* 4 artichoke
  hearts, quartered

Combine all ingredients and toss together lightly.

Of Radishes and Things
(Serves 2)

8–10 leaves of leaf or red
  lettuce, torn
8–10 leaves of spinach or
  romaine leaves, torn

6–10 radishes, sliced in thin
  rounds
½ cucumber, chopped

Mix and serve with a favourite dressing.

Beet Treat Salad
(Serves 2–4)

1 avocado, chopped
6–8 large lettuce leaves (leaf, red, romaine, bibb or Boston), torn
1 green bell pepper, sliced in rings or trips

¼–½ cup lentil, mung, alfalfa or other sprouts, hulls removed
2–4 beets, grated

Toss all the ingredients together *except* for the beets. Dish out the salad and spread the beets over the top. Serve with lemon juice or **Lemon Herb Dressing** for the best flavour.

Super Sprout Salad
(Serves 2–4)

1 cup alfalfa sprouts
1 cup other sprouts
8–14 spinach leaves, torn
½ red bell pepper, cut in strips or chopped

¼ cup (or less) broccoli florets, tips only, broken very small
Optional: 1–2 tomatoes, cut in thin wedges or chopped *or* 6–8 radishes, sliced thin

Be sure to choose very fresh sprouts for the best flavour and digestibility. To make them more digestible and avoid their carcinogenic properties, rinse them very thoroughly to remove *all* the brown hulls. Toss gently with all the other ingredients and serve with your favourite dressing.

Zucchini Ribbon Salad
(Serves 4)

2–3 small fresh zucchini
2 or more cups assorted
   mixed greens (endive,
   cress, lettuce, spinach,
   arugula, sorrel, wild
   greens and/or sprouts)

cherry tomatoes

Choose bright green, firm zucchini for the best flavour. Use a potato peeler to cut thin strips of ribbons from one end of the zucchini to the other. Arrange these in artistic curls on a bed of mixed greens and top with one or more cherry tomatoes. Serve with an oil-and-herb dressing to accent the greens.

Wild Green Salad
(Serves 2)

1 cup wild or mixed special
   greens (arugula, sorrel,
   cress, lamb's quarters, red
   oak, young dandelions
   and/or mint leaves, etc.)
½–1 small Boston or bibb
   lettuce, torn

4 artichoke hearts,
   quartered, *or* 8–16 olives,
   whole or sliced
1 tomato, cut in chunks *or* 1
   red, purple or yellow bell
   pepper, cut in strips

Toss everything together and serve with a favourite dressing.

Eat Your Flowers!

For decades health advocates have been interested in bee products, including honey, pollen, propolis and royal jelly. What has often been overlooked is the source of these products, which is nectar and pollen from flowers.

Since veganism has become an ecological and humanitarian trend that is here to stay, it is only logical that we would want a firsthand food and nutrient source from flowers rather than from commercial beekeeping, where bees are overworked only to be robbed of their honey and often fed sugar water instead.

Longevity specialists have long been aware that so-called primitive tribes have thrived on the regular consumption of flowers in their diets. The healthy Hunzas include flowers as a part of their food supply every day. Many country people in Europe and elsewhere have for centuries used flowers as food and medicine. The wildflower heads (stamens and petals) have been picked and chewed for their juices and fragrance. Everything from soup to jam has been made from flowers.

Most flowers are high in vitamin C, bioflavinoids and trace minerals. There are also special nutritional substances found in flowers which are not found in any other food sources. Many (like chamomile, passion flowers and hops) have a calming effect on the nerves. Some flowers (like red clover) are mild blood purifiers, while others (like calendula, marigold and honeysuckle) are good for infections.

In Chinese medicine, flowers are considered to have "cooling" or "yin" properties.

Some tasty, wholesome wildflower varieties: pea vetches, wild rose petals and violets, Indian paintbrush, some lilies (day, wood and chocolate), ocean spray, red clover, chamomile and alfalfa flowers. Cultivated, edible flowers include pansies, nasturtiums, bachelor buttons, marigolds, dianthus, calendula, carnations, and borage, thyme and chive blossoms. Also try cooked flowers like marsh marigolds. Garden squash flowers are also excellent in a stir-fry.

Be sure to check blossoms carefully when picking flowers in the wild, as not all wildflowers are edible! If you wish to grow your own flowers, purchase seeds as natural as possible and keep them in a garden away from the roadside and pesticides or artificial fertilizers and sprays. Be very careful not to consume just any garden flowers. Besides the fact that some flowers are poisonous, edible flowers grown incorrectly could be toxic rather than beneficial to your health.

Susan, a local B.C. edible-flower seller I know, has this to say about flowers: "Eating flowers gives you a sense of reverence for what you are eating. People slow down their eating and appreciate the food more."

I must admit, I agree. If we can slow down our lives a little more to admire (and savour) the flowers, we may find we enjoy life's beauties much more fully. The taste of life is sweet!

Flowers and Wild Greens Salad

| Handful of edible flowers | Wild greens: lambs' quarters, young dandelions, mint leaves and/or sorrel, cress, arugula, red oak, etc. |

Toss gently in **Herbs and Oil Dressing**.

Great Grated Salad
(Serves 2–4)

1 small zucchini, grated
1 large or 2 small carrots,
    grated fine
1–2 new potatoes with skins,
    grated, *or* 1 small, fresh
    turnip or parsnip, *or* 3–4
    Jerusalem artichokes,
    grated

3–4 cauliflower florets,
    grated
Optional: 1–2 stalks
    broccoli—just the
    stalks—peeled and grated
Optional: 2 or more cherry
    tomatoes
1 small fresh beet, grated

Toss all the ingredients together, *except* for the beet (it will dye everything red!). Serve the salad in bowls and sprinkle beet in a circle around the edge of each bowl. Top with one or more cherry tomatoes for added eye appeal if desired. A creamy dressing tastes best with this salad.

Avocado Stuffed with Marinated Vegetables
(Serves 2–4)

1–2 medium or large
    avocados, cut in half and
    pitted
Spinach *or* lettuce leaves

**Marinated Vegetable
Medley** (including
tomatoes, mushrooms
and cucumber)

Cut ripe avocados in half, peel them with a butter knife or leave them in the skins. Place them on a bed of fresh spinach or leafy lettuce. Stuff each half with fully marinated vegetables and serve as a salad or side dish or as a snack. An elegant treat.

Avocado Boats
(Serves 2)

1 large avocado, cut in half,
  unpeeled
1 Tbsp. almonds *or*
  hazelnuts (filberts)
1 Tbsp. cashew pieces *or*
  pecans

1 Tbsp. sunflower seeds
Optional: ½–1 Tbsp. raisins
  or currants
Optional: 2 tsp. shredded
  unsweetened coconut

Scoop 1–2 Tbsp. of avocado out of each half to make room for the
filling, and eat it or use it in other recipes. Combine the remaining
ingredients and fill up each avocado half. Place the avocado halves
on a bed of lettuce or spinach with extra nuts on the side if desired.
Top each with soy yogurt, a creamy dressing or sesame tahini, or
nut butter thinned with nut milk. Enjoy this delightful little salad
as a change from traditional green, leafy salads.

Wild Zucchini Rice Salad
(Serves 2–4)

½ cup mixed dry wild rice
  and dry brown rice
1–2 small zucchini, grated
1 tomato, cut in wedges or
  chunks

1 red, yellow or purple bell
  pepper, cut in strips
½ bunch of spinach or less,
  torn small
1 avocado, cut in chunks

Cook the dry rice (it makes about 1 cup cooked), and cool or chill.
Mix all the ingredients together and toss in a favourite dressing.
This makes a great meal for two or a prelude to a meal for four.

Millet or Quinoa Salad

Choose any leafy green salad as a base for this recipe. Add ½–1 cup cooked and cooled millet or quinoa, and ½ cup or more of nuts or seeds if desired. Toss all the ingredients in an oil or creamy dressing and enjoy. Nuts are best if chopped or soaked in water ½–1 hour before using.

Greek Salad
(Serves 2)

2 tomatoes, cut in chunks
½ cucumber, cut in
   quarters, then chopped
1 green bell pepper, cut in
   1" chunks

½–¾ cup black olives, cut in
   half lengthwise
Optional: ¼–½ red onion,
   chopped small

Mix everything together and toss in an oil-based dressing, preferably one with olive oil. If possible, let the salad and dressing marinate together in the fridge 15–30 minutes before the meal. Stir once while marinating. Enjoy with crusty bread.

Italian Pasta Salad

4–6 oz rotini (spiral noodles)
Dressing:
2 Tbsp. chopped fresh
  parsley
¼ tsp *each* oregano, basil,
  vegetable powder, sea salt
  and paprika
3 Tbsp. olive oil
2 Tbsp. red wine vinegar or
  other vinegar
1–2 tsp. tamari soy sauce
Optional: 1 clove garlic,
  pressed

2 tomatoes, cored and
  chopped
1 cup broccoli florets, lightly
  steamed
10–20 black olives, sliced in
  half
10–20 spinach leaves, torn
¼–½ cup chopped green
  onions *and/or* sliced
  mushrooms

Bring 2 quarts water to a boil and add the pasta. Cook 6–8 minutes, keeping the water boiling, until firm (*al dente*) or however you like it. While the pasta is cooking, prepare the dressing. Add the seasonings to the wet ingredients and mix thoroughly. Prepare the vegetables. Steam the broccoli. When the pasta is ready, drain in a colander and rinse completely with cold water. Add the pasta and vegetables to the dressing and toss well. Serve and enjoy as a meal or side dish. Keeps several days refrigerated.

Oriental Salad
(Serves 2)

8–10 stalks asparagus, steamed 6–8 minutes until tender

10–14 snow peas (edible pea pods), trimmed

1 small carrot, cut in shoestrings (see below)

1 small stalk celery, cut in shoestrings

1 small can or ½ large can bamboo shoots, rinsed and dried

½ can water chestnuts, sliced thin

Optional: green onions *or* chives, chopped

Optional: 1–2 Tbsp. raw or toasted sesame seeds *or* **Home Roasted Almonds**, sliced

Steam the asparagus. To cut vegetables into shoestrings, chop into 2½" lengths, then slice into very thin, long sticks. Toss all ingredients together and marinate for 1–2 hours before serving in fresh lemon juice, **Lemon Herb Dressing** or **Herbs and Oil Dressing**. This salad is especially nice when it is artistically arranged on a plate.

Perfect Potato Salad

(Serves 4–6)

5 cups chopped, unpeeled
  potatoes
Marinade:
½ cup oil or water
3 Tbsp. apple cider vinegar
1–2 tsp. dried parsley,
  crushed
¼ tsp. *each* basil and sea salt
Several dashes *each* cayenne
  pepper and sea kelp

⅓–½ cup chopped fresh
  parsley
½ cup eggless or tofu
  mayonnaise, or more to
  taste
½ tsp. paprika
¼–½ tsp. powdered
  horseradish, or to taste, *or*
  3–6 green onions,
  chopped fine
Sea salt *or* vegetable sea salt
  to taste
Several dashes cayenne
  pepper
Optional: ½ tsp. celery seed

Choose thin-skinned brown potatoes. Chop and steam them until
very tender. Marinate the potatoes in the marinade for 2–4 hours
or overnight in the refrigerator, stirring every half hour, or 3–4
times. Drain off excess liquid, if any, and mix the potatoes with all
the other ingredients. Chill thoroughly for 1 hour or more before
serving.

Dressings

Herbs and Oil Dressing

1¼ cups safflower oil, sunflower oil, or other natural oil
¼ cup apple cider vinegar
1 Tbsp. dried parsley flakes, crushed
1 tsp. *each* sea salt, paprika and tamari soy sauce
½ tsp. basil

¼ tsp. *each* sea kelp, marjoram and thyme
Several dashes cayenne pepper
Optional: ½–1 tsp. vegetable broth powder
Optional: 2–3 Tbsp. flax or pumpkin oil

Mix or beat the ingredients together well and refrigerate for a couple of hours so the flavours can mingle. Beat or shake the mixture a few times as it chills. Serve chilled on all kinds of leafy green and sprout salads. Keeps refrigerated for 2 weeks or longer.

Lemon Herb Dressing

Follow the directions for **Herbs and Oil Dressing** (above) but omit the vinegar and tamari soy sauce. Instead, add 2–4 Tbsp. fresh lemon juice and increase the sea salt to 1¼ tsp. if desired. Blend in 2 green onions or 1–2 cloves garlic for added flavour, to taste.

Cucumber Dill Dressing

1 large cucumber, peeled
and seeded
2 tsp. dill weed
½ cup oil *and/or* water
(some loss of flavour with
water)

Several dashes *each* cayenne
pepper and sea kelp
Sea salt to taste
Optional: 1–2 cloves garlic,
crushed

Blend all ingredients well, chill and serve. Best used within 5 days. Use ¼–½ cup flax oil for extra nutrients and a surprisingly nice flavour. This is a great dressing for low-fat diets if some water is used.

Avocado Dressing

2 ripe, medium avocados
3–4 tsp. chopped fresh
parsley
¼ cup safflower, sunflower
or other natural oil
¼ cup fresh lemon juice *or*
extra oil

¼ tsp. horseradish or onion
powder, or to taste
⅛–¼ tsp. sea salt
Few dashes sea kelp
Cayenne pepper to taste
Optional: 1 tsp. toasted
sesame oil

Blend all ingredients together well and correct seasonings to taste. Chill and serve on salads or vegetables. Keeps refrigerated for up to 3 days.

Tahini Tofu Dressing

6 oz (175 g) tofu, crumbled
½ cup sesame tahini
5–6 Tbsp. water
4–5 Tbsp. sunflower,
  safflower, flax or
  pumpkin oil
½–⅔ cup freshly squeezed
  lemon juice
2 Tbsp. chopped fresh
  parsley *or* 1 Tbsp. dried
  parsley, crushed

1 tsp. prepared horseradish
  or 1–3 green onions,
  chopped
½ tsp. *each* paprika and sea
  salt
⅛ tsp. sea kelp
Cayenne pepper to taste
Optional: 1 tsp. toasted
  sesame oil

Use a food processor or blender to combine all ingredients together well. Serve immediately or chill before using, as a salad dressing or vegetable dip. Keeps 2–4 days refrigerated.

Creamy Onion Dressing

6 oz (175 g) tofu, crumbled
⅓–⅔ cup milk substitute
4–7 green onions, chopped
  fine
2–4 tsp. ground raw cashews
  or blanched almonds
2 tsp. tamari soy sauce

1–2 tsp. parsley
½ tsp. *each* basil and paprika
Sea salt *or* vegetable sea salt
  to taste
Optional: bit of liquid
  sweetener

Combine all ingredients in a blender, reserving some of the chopped green onion tops. Stir them in after blending and add liquid sweetener to taste. Chill before serving. Keeps 4–7 days refrigerated.

Garlic French Dressing

1 cup natural light oil
⅓ cup **Natural Ketchup**
¼–⅓ cup apple cider vinegar
1–2 cloves garlic, crushed
1 Tbsp. liquid sweetener

1 tsp. sea salt
1 tsp. paprika
Several dashes cayenne
  pepper

Blend or beat all the ingredients together. Chill and serve.

Zesty Tomato Dressing

1–1½ cups tomatoes,
  peeled, seeded and
  chopped *or* 1¼ cups
  tomato juice
½ cup natural oil
1–3 green onions, chopped
1 Tbsp. apple cider vinegar
  or 1–2 Tbsp. fresh lemon
  juice

1–2 tsp. liquid sweetener
1 tsp. sea salt, or to taste
1 tsp. parsley
½ tsp. *each* paprika and dill
  weed
¼ tsp. *each* basil and oregano
Several dashes *each* cayenne
  pepper and sea kelp

Blend all ingredients until smooth and chill before serving. Keeps
7 or more days refrigerated.

Special Italian Dressing

1 cup natural oil
¼–⅓ cup apple cider vinegar
1–2 green onions, chopped
¼–½ green pepper, chopped
1–2 sprigs parsley *or* 1–1½
   tsp. dried parsley
1 clove garlic, minced

1 Tbsp. lemon juice
1 tsp. sea salt *or* vegetable
   sea salt
½ tsp. *each* basil, marjoram,
   anise seed and dill weed
⅛ tsp. cayenne pepper

Combine all the ingredients in a blender and blend for 2 minutes until smooth. Chill before serving if desired.

Citrus Sauce #1

¼ cup natural oil
2 Tbsp. fresh orange juice
1 Tbsp. fresh lemon juice

¼ tsp. finely grated orange
   rind
Optional: few dashes sea salt

Mix everything together and use as a sauce or dip for artichokes or other green vegetables. Can also be used as a salad dressing.

Citrus Sauce #2

1–2 Tbsp. natural oil
2–3 Tbsp. fresh lemon juice

Several dashes sea salt

Mix everything together and use as a sauce or dip for artichokes or other green vegetables. Can also be used as a salad dressing.

Soups

Easy Asparagus Soup
(Serves 1)

1 medium bunch asparagus
(about 2 cups chopped)
¼ cup water *or* milk
substitute
½–1 small clove garlic

1–1½ tsp. tamari soy sauce
or miso *or* 1 vegetable
bouillon cube
½ tsp. vegetable sea salt
Couple dashes *each* cayenne
pepper and sea kelp

Break the top two-thirds of the asparagus into 2–3 small pieces. Remove and discard all the white parts of the stalks on the remaining asparagus. Peel the leftover green parts to remove the stringy, hard-to-digest parts. Steam asparagus until tender. Blend all the ingredients together until smooth.* Add a bit of extra liquid if desired. Put the mixture in a covered saucepan and cook on medium-low heat for 20–25 minutes until hot throughout and the garlic flavour becomes more subtle.

*The garlic may be sautéed in advance if desired, although it is preferable not to add oil to this healing, green recipe.

Quick Broccoli or Zucchini Soup
(Serves 2–3)

4½–5 cups chopped
  broccoli *or* zucchini
1 cup water *or* milk substitute
½–1 small clove garlic
3 tsp. tamari soy sauce *or*
  miso

1–1½ tsp. vegetable sea salt
1 tsp. parsley
½ tsp. basil
Couple dashes *each* cayenne
  pepper and sea kelp

Pick firm, bright green stalks of broccoli for the tastiest soup. Avoid limp, purplish or yellowish florets and thick stalks. Cut ½"–1" off the bottom of each broccoli stalk and discard it. Cut the remaining broccoli in half, one half being stalk and the other half broccoli florets. Peel the stem part and discard peelings. Chop the rest of the stem into rounds. Chop the top part of the broccoli into trees. Steam all until tender.

If zucchini is used, choose firm, bright green and white squash. Avoid yellowish or dark green zucchini as they are bitter. Cut ¼" off each zucchini end and discard. Cut the rest into ¼" rounds and steam until tender.

Blend all ingredients together and cook on medium-low heat for 20–25 minutes until hot throughout and the flavours mingle. See **Easy Asparagus Soup** for other variations.

Miso Soup
(Serves 6–8)

1 tsp. regular or toasted
  sesame oil
2–3 green onions, chopped
  small

4 cups water *or* stock
¼ cup dark miso

1 Tbsp. tamari soy sauce
⅛ tsp. sea kelp
Cayenne pepper to taste
2–3 oz (50–60 g) regular
  tofu, diced into ⅛" cubes
Optional: 10–16 leaves
  spinach *or* chard, chopped

Heat the oil and sauté the green onion until tender, then add all the remaining ingredients *except* the tofu and greens. Use a wire whisk to help mix in the miso while stirring over medium-low heat. When the miso has dissolved, add the tofu and greens and let everything simmer on low heat for 8–12 minutes until the greens are tender. Correct the seasonings as desired. Serve hot. Keeps 3–6 days refrigerated. Do not freeze. Don't allow the soup to boil at any time, especially while reheating.

Garden Vegetable Soup
(Serves 4–5)

4–6 large tomatoes, cored and chopped *or* 1 large can (28 oz/796 mL) tomatoes, cored and chopped with juice

2 green peppers, chopped

½ large or 2 small bunches spinach, lightly chopped

2–4 green onions, chopped small

1 large carrot, diced or quartered and sliced

1 cup water *or* stock

2 vegetable bouillon cubes *or* 1–2 tsp. vegetable broth powder

3 tsp. parsley

¼ tsp. sea kelp

Vegetable sea salt and cayenne pepper to taste

Mix all the ingredients together and bring to a quick boil. Turn down the heat immediately and simmer on low to medium heat for about 25–35 minutes until the vegetables are tender and the flavours mingle. Serve and enjoy. Keeps refrigerated 3–5 days.

Blended Garden Vegetable Soup

Add ½–1 large or 2 small beets along with the other vegetables in **Garden Vegetable Soup** (above). Proceed with the recipe as directed above, but blend the soup until smooth before serving.

Healing Greens Soup
(Serves 2–3)

3–5 bunches mixed greens: spinach, beet greens, chard, kale and/or mustard greens (about 3–3½ cups cooked)

4–6 green onions, tops only, chopped

1 cup nut milk, rice milk or soy milk

1–2 tsp. maple syrup *or* rice syrup

1–1½ tsp. vegetable sea salt

1 tsp. vegetable broth powder *or* 1 vegetable bouillon cube

2–3 dashes powdered ginger *or* bit of fresh squeezed ginger juice

Choose firm, bright or dark green leaves. Remove any blemishes. Wash the greens carefully to remove grit and sand. Leave the stems on the greens and chop lightly. Steam the greens until tender. Blend the cooked greens with all the remaining ingredients. Simmer on medium-low heat for 15–20 minutes until hot throughout. Enjoy this hearty soup, rich in iron and minerals.

Magnificent Mushroom Cashew Soup
(Serves 2–3)

2 cups chopped mushrooms

1 small onion, chopped small (about ¾ cup)

2½ Tbsp. natural oil

½ cup ground "raw" cashew pieces

1–1¼ cups water *or* stock

1–2 vegetable bouillon cubes

Vegetable sea salt and cayenne pepper to taste

1–2 dashes sea kelp

¼ cup whole "raw" cashew pieces

Sauté 1 cup of the mushrooms with the onion in 1½ Tbsp. of the oil until tender. Blend the sautéed vegetables with the ground cashew pieces, water, bouillon cubes, sea salt, cayenne pepper and sea kelp. Heat the remaining oil and sauté the whole cashew pieces and remaining 1 cup mushrooms until tender. Add this to the blended mixture and bring just to a boil on low to medium heat. Simmer everything on low heat for 10–20 minutes until hot throughout and the flavours mingle. This is an exquisite soup and one of my personal favourites. Keeps several days refrigerated.

Elegant Chestnut Soup
(Serves 4)

3 cups fresh, whole chestnuts (about 45–50 medium or large), roasted and peeled

1 Tbsp. natural or natural light oil

½ cup finely chopped white or yellow onion

1 stalk celery, chopped small (about ½ cup)

2¼ cups water

¾ cup apple juice *or* sweet cider*

1–2 tsp. tamari *or* miso*

1 vegetable boulllon cube

Optional: 1–2 dashes nutmeg

To prepare chestnuts, see **Roasted Chestnuts**. Peel off the outer shell and the fuzzy skin before using the inner chestnut meat.

Heat the oil until hot and sauté the onion until semi-tender. Add the celery and sauté until both are very tender. Blend the water and apple juice with the chestnuts and all the remaining ingredients. Simmer everything on low to medium heat (do *not* boil!) for about 15–20 minutes or until hot throughout and the flavours mingle. Enjoy this rich and tantalizing soup with extra chopped or ground nuts as a garnish. Keeps 4–6 days refrigerated.

*Two vegetable bouillon cubes can be used instead of the tamari or miso. Also, ½ cup applesauce and 2½ cups water can be used instead of the juice and 2¼ cups water.

Easy Chestnut Soup
(Serves 6–7)

1½ cups dried chestnuts (from Oriental food stores)
6 cups water

1 cup chopped onion
2 cups chopped mushrooms (Shitake are best)
4–6 tsp. natural oil

½ cup ground raw cashews, blanched almonds, hazelnuts (filberts) *or* Brazil nuts
⅔–1 cup water *or* stock
2–3 tsp. sweetener
1–2 vegetable bouillon cubes
¾–1 tsp. sea salt
½ tsp. cinnamon
2–3 dashes nutmeg
Several dashes cayenne pepper

Rinse the chestnuts thoroughly and put them in a pot with three cups of water. Cover the pan and bring to a boil on high heat. Turn off the heat when they boil. Let them sit, covered, for 2–3 hours to absorb water and expand. Then rinse the chestnuts thoroughly and add 3 more cups water to the pot with the chestnuts. Bring them to a boil again and let them sit 1 hour. Once again rinse thoroughly with water, many times, to lessen their odour.

While the chestnuts are soaking for the second time, sauté the onions until semi-tender, then add the mushrooms and sauté until both are fully tender. Blend the sautéed mixture with the chestnuts and all the remaining ingredients. Correct seasonings to taste. Enjoy with extra ground toasted nuts and chopped green onions or chives if desired. This recipe is not as fancy as the **Elegant Chestnut Soup**, but it is easier as it saves peeling all those chestnuts. Enjoy this hearty soup any time of year, especially when fresh chestnuts are unavailable. Keeps 4–6 days refrigerated. May be frozen.

Spring Green Onion Soup
(Serves 6)

4 cups potatoes, chopped
  small *or* 3–3½ cups
  packed, cooked brown
  rice or other cooked
  whole grain
1½ cups celery, chopped
  (about 4 stalks)
2 bunches (about 15–18)
  green onions, chopped
  (about 2½ cups)
2–3 Tbsp. natural oil
2 vegetable bouillon cubes

3–5 tsp. tamari soy sauce *or*
  miso
3–4 tsp. parsley
1–2 tsp. liquid sweetener (to
  balance flavours)
1½ tsp. paprika
1 tsp. *each* sea salt, dill weed
  and thyme
Several dashes *each* cayenne
  pepper and sea kelp
Optional: ½–1 tsp. vegetable
  broth powder
2½ cups water *or* stock

Steam the potatoes and celery until tender. In a large frying pan, sauté the green onion in the oil for 1–2 minutes, then add all the seasonings and sauté 1 more minute. Filling the blender twice, blend all the ingredients until a fairly smooth, lovely light green soup is created. Simmer everything on low to medium heat for 15–25 minutes until the bite is off the onions and the flavours mingle. Serve hot with bread, crackers or other accompaniments. Keeps 3–6 days refrigerated.

Tomato Rice Soup
(Serves 8–10)

1 small onion, chopped
⅔ cup chopped celery
 (about 2 stalks)
3 Tbsp. natural oil
10–12 large tomatoes,
 peeled, cored, seeded and
 finely chopped *or* 2 - 28 oz
 (796 mL) cans tomatoes
 and their juice (core and
 crush the tomatoes and
 strain the juice)
1 vegetable bouillon cube *or*
 1 tsp. vegetable broth
 powder

2 tsp. tamari soy sauce *or*
 miso
1 tsp. liquid sweetener
¾–1 tsp. sea salt
½ tsp. paprika
Several dashes *each* cayenne
 pepper and sea kelp
Optional (if canned tomatoes
 are used above): 1–2 fresh
 tomatoes, peeled and
 chopped

1–1½ cups thick nut milk
1 cup cooked brown rice
 (about ½ cup dry)

Sauté the onion and celery in the oil until slightly tender. Add the tomatoes and simmer on low heat, covered, for 30–40 minutes until the tomatoes are very tender and no longer taste acidic. Then add the herbs and remaining ingredients, *except* the milk and rice, and cook another 10–15 minutes.

Cool the mixture slightly and blend it with the milk, using less milk for a richer, redder soup and more for a milder, creamier soup. Add the cooked rice and heat the soup to just under the boiling point. Serve hot, garnished with fresh parsley, green onions or chives. Keeps refrigerated 5–7 days. Avoid freezing.

Hearty Vegetable Soup
(Serves 8–10)

2 medium potatoes,
  unpeeled and cut into
  small chunks *or* ¾–1 cup
  alphabets or other small
  noodles
2–3 carrots, chopped or
  thinly sliced
1 medium stalk broccoli,
  chopped

1 very large onion, chopped
  small
2 cups chopped mushrooms
  or peeled, finely chopped
  eggplant
2 Tbsp. natural oil

6 cups water *or* vegetable
  stock

4–6 large tomatoes *or* 1 large
  can (28 oz/796 mL)
  tomatoes, cored and
  chopped
3–4 stalks celery, chopped
1 small zucchini, quartered
  and chopped
Optional: 1 green, red or
  other bell pepper,
  chopped
1–2 Tbsp. tamari soy sauce
2–3 tsp. vegetable broth
  powder *or* 2 vegetable
  bouillon cubes
2–3 tsp. dried parsley *or* ¼
  cup chopped fresh parsley
1–1½ tsp. sea salt
½ tsp. *each* basil, oregano
  and sea kelp
Cayenne pepper to taste
Optional: 1–2 tsp. sweetener
  (to balance flavours)

Steam the potatoes, carrots and broccoli for 6–8 minutes before
making the soup.

Sauté the onions and mushrooms or eggplant in the oil in a
large pot until they are slightly transparent. (Use an extra 1 Tbsp.
oil if eggplant is used.) Add the water or stock, steamed vegetables
and remaining vegetables, and cook 30 minutes longer on
medium-low heat until the vegetables are tender but not soggy and
the flavours have developed.

Add the sea salt and herbs and correct according to taste.

Cornucopia Soup
(Serves 4–6)

6–7 cups water *or* stock
½ cup brown pot barley
¼ cup red lentils
2 cups chopped cabbage
2 stalks celery, chopped small
3 large carrots, sliced ¼"
    thick
1 small stalk broccoli,
    chopped
2 cloves garlic, chopped
½ small onion, chopped
5–6 mushrooms, sliced
1 cup lightly chopped
    spinach

½ small zucchini, quartered
    and chopped small
2 Tbsp. tamari soy sauce *or*
    miso
3–4 tsp. parsley
1 tsp. *each* sea salt, basil,
    thyme and paprika
2 tsp. vegetable broth
    powder *or* 2 vegetable
    bouillon cubes
¼ tsp. sea kelp
Several dashes cayenne
    pepper
Optional: 2–3 tsp. liquid
    sweetener

Heat the water, barley and lentils on high heat until they boil, then reduce the heat to medium. Cook for 15 minutes, then add the cabbage, celery, carrots and broccoli. Cook another 15 minutes, then add all the remaining ingredients except for the garlic and onion. Cook for 15 minutes longer. Remove 2–3 cups of broth and vegetables from the soup and blend them with the raw garlic and onion. Add the blended mixture back to the soup and simmer everything on medium-low heat for a final 15–20 minutes, until the flavours mingle and the sharp edge of the onion and garlic become subtle.

This robust yet light soup is especially nice on a cool day. Different vegetables can be substituted as desired.

Seaweed Soup
(Serves 4–6)

2 Tbsp. natural oil
1 large onion, chopped
2 carrots, thinly sliced
3–4 stalks celery, chopped
6 cups water *or* stock
1–2 oz dried seaweed *or* 4 oz fresh (wakame or kombu are best), rinsed and sliced

1–2 vegetable bouillon cubes *or* 1–2 tsp. vegetable broth powder
2–3 tsp. parsley
½ tsp. sea salt
Several dashes sea kelp

⅓ cup dark miso (brown rice or soy miso are good)

Heat the oil in a pot big enough to hold all the soup. Add the onions and vegetables and sauté. When the vegetables are tender and the onions are slightly transparent, add the water, seaweed and all the rest of the soup ingredients *except* the miso. Let the soup cook, covered, for about 25–35 minutes.

Remove the soup from the heat, take 1 cup of broth from the pot and stir the miso into this broth. When the miso is dissolved, return the broth to the soup pot. Let it stand, covered and away from the heat, for 5–10 minutes so the flavours can mingle. Do not cook the miso; this destroys valuable minerals and enzymes. Serve the soup immediately when ready. Leftover soup can be reheated gently, but never let it boil. Keeps refrigerated 5–6 days. Do not freeze.

Adzuki or Pinto Bean Soup
(Serves 10–12)

2 cups dry adzuki beans *or* pinto beans, soaked and cooked (2 cups dry beans makes about 5 cups cooked)

10 cups water *or* stock

1 large onion, finely chopped (about 2 cups)

2–3 Tbsp. tamari soy sauce

1–2 Tbsp. parsley

2 Tbsp. natural oil

4 tsp. vegetable broth powder

2 vegetable bouillon cubes

½–1 tsp. sea salt *or* vegetable sea salt

½–¾ tsp. sea kelp

Cayenne pepper to taste

Optional: 1–2 tsp. sweetener (to balance flavours)

3–4 Tbsp. dark miso

Cook the adzuki or pinto beans until very tender. After cooking, add enough water or stock to make a total of 10 cups of liquid. Add the onion and cook on low to medium heat for 20 minutes. Then add the remaining ingredients *except* the miso, and cook 20 minutes more on medium heat.

Take 2–4 cups of beans and liquid from the soup, blend or process into liquid, and return it to the soup. Next, take out 1 more cup of the liquid from the soup and mix the miso into it, stirring it carefully to break down any lumps, then return the miso liquid to the soup.

1–2 cups hot water may be added to the soup after adding the miso if a thinner, milder soup is desired. Serve hot and enjoy this easy-to-digest, highly nutritious soup. Keeps 7–8 days refrigerated and freezes wonderfully.

Hot and Sour Soup*
(Serves 6)

8 dried Chinese mushrooms

8 cups vegetable stock
8 slices dried galangal (Thai
  ginger) *or* regular ginger,
  peeled
½ lime, peeled and sliced
  thin
4 Tbsp. lime juice

1 Tbsp. lemon juice
2 Tbsp. Japanese light soy
  sauce
2 fresh red and green chilies
  (serrano are best)
1 lb (450 g) firm tofu, in
  small chunks
Chopped fresh cilantro

Rinse the mushrooms, put them in a small saucepan and cover with water. Bring them to a boil on high heat and swish the mushrooms to remove excess dirt. Discard the water. Rinse. Once again cover the mushrooms and bring them to a boil, covered. Let sit 1 hour. Then drain, remove tough stems, squeeze out excess water and slice or cut in half.

Bring the stock to a boil in a large saucepan on high heat, add the ginger and lime slices and cook for 2–3 minutes. Lower the heat and add the lime and lemon juice, soy sauce and chilies. Simmer for 5 minutes. Add the tofu and mushrooms and simmer 5 more minutes. Taste to check the balance of hot, sour and salt—none should overwhelm the other—and add more chilies, lime juice or soy sauce as needed. Serve garnished with chopped cilantro. Have a side dish of extra sliced chilies for those who like it hot. Keeps a few days refrigerated but is best served fresh.

*Original recipe by David Tinker, Vancouver chef.

Winter Squash and Apple Soup*
(Serves 6)

2 cups butternut or
buttercup squash, peeled,
seeded and chopped
2 cups sweet potato, peeled
and chopped
3 medium apples, peeled,
cored and chopped
(spartan, Macintosh or
similar cooking apple)

1 medium onion, chopped
2 cups water, or just enough
to cover apples and
veggies
½ tsp. sea salt
½ tsp. Chinese 5-spice *or*
pumpkin pie spice
¼ tsp. cayenne pepper

Bring the vegetables, apples and water to a boil in a saucepan on high heat. Reduce the heat and simmer 30 minutes, or until all the vegetables are tender. Add the seasonings and use a blender to process the mixture. Heat in the saucepan again on low heat until hot. Keeps 3–5 days refrigerated.

*Original recipe by David Tinker, Vancouver chef.

Sauces and Gravies

Mushroom Gravy
(Makes 2½ cups)

1 cup mushrooms, sliced thin
1 Tbsp. natural oil*
1¾ cups water
⅓–½ cup flour: whole
    wheat, kamut, spelt, millet
    or quinoa
2–3 Tbsp. tamari soy sauce
    or dark miso

1–2 tsp. vegetable broth
    powder *or* 1–2 vegetable
    bouillon cubes
Several dashes sea kelp
Optional: sea salt or
    vegetable sea salt, to taste

Sauté the mushrooms in the oil. Add the flour and stir constantly over medium-low heat for 1–2 minutes to brown the flour for more flavour. Add the remaining ingredients and stir with a wire whisk until the sauce is well mixed and there are no lumps. Stir constantly over medium heat until very hot. Reduce heat and cook on the lowest setting for 10–15 minutes until the sauce is thickened. Stir occasionally while simmering.

Serve over hot vegetables, burgers, balls or whole grains and enjoy!

*To eliminate oil from this recipe, sauté the mushrooms in the tamari or a bit of the water instead.

117

Vegetarian Gravy
(Makes 2½ cups)

2 cups kidney, pinto or
    adzuki bean cooking juice
2–3 Tbsp. tamari soy sauce
    or dark miso
1 Tbsp. natural oil
⅓ cup whole wheat, kamut,
    millet or quinoa flour

¼–½ tsp. chili powder,
    vegetable broth powder *or*
    curry powder
¼ tsp. sea salt *or* vegetable
    sea salt
¼ tsp. sea kelp
Several dashes cayenne
    pepper

Use previously stored frozen bean juice, or cook ½–1 lb (225–450 g) beans until very tender and drain off and save 2 cups of the liquid. Use the "muddiest" part of the liquid for this recipe. Use the beans in another recipe, or freeze them for later use.

    Combine all the remaining ingredients with the cooled bean juice and stir over medium-low heat until thickened. Use a wire whisk or blender to mix well. Correct the seasonings to taste, and serve the gravy on potatoes, rice, whole grains, vegetables, mock meat loaf, burgers and other dishes.

Creamy Cashew Sauce
(Makes 2 cups)

1 cup "raw" cashew pieces,
    ground
1¼ cups water
2 Tbsp. arrowroot powder *or*
    other thickener
2–3 tsp. liquid sweetener

¾–1 tsp. sea salt
⅛ tsp. nutmeg, or more to
    taste
⅛ tsp. sea kelp
¼–⅓ cup "raw" cashew
    pieces, left whole

Grind the cashews ¼ cup at a time in the blender, or all at once in a food processor. Put all the ingredients into a blender *except* for the ¼–⅓ cup whole cashew pieces. Blend at high speed until liquefied. Place the mixture in a saucepan or double boiler with the whole cashew pieces and stir over medium-low heat until thickened and hot throughout. Serve over green and/or yellow vegetables with a bed of whole grains underneath if desired. Also use for **Fantastic Fondues**, burgers and balls. Keeps 6–8 days or more refrigerated.

Toasted Cashew Sauce
(Makes 3 cups)

1½ cups "raw" cashew pieces
2 cups water
1–2 Tbsp. arrowroot powder
   or other thickener
2 Tbsp. chopped white onion
1 clove garlic, crushed
1 Tbsp. tamari soy sauce

2–3 tsp. peeled, grated
   ginger root
Sea salt to taste
Few dashes cayenne pepper
   to taste
Optional: 1 vegetable
   bouillon cube

Spread the cashews about ¼" thick on a shallow baking dish or pie pan. Bake for 10–15 minutes at 300°F, stirring once. Blend the cashews ¼ cup at a time in the blender until finely ground. Add all the ingredients to the blender and liquefy. Heat the sauce on medium-low heat, stirring regularly. When thickened and hot throughout, serve over vegetables, grains or other main dishes. Keeps 6–8 days refrigerated.

Toasted Sesame Sauce
(Makes 3½ cups)

1 cup toasted, hulled sesame
  seeds, ground
1 cup tahini
2 cups water *or* milk
  substitute
2 Tbsp. arrowroot powder *or*
  other thickener
1–2 Tbsp. chopped white
  onion

1 clove garlic, crushed
1 Tbsp. tamari soy sauce
1 vegetable bouillon cube
2–3 tsp. lemon rind, grated
Sea salt to taste
Few dashes cayenne pepper
  to taste

Spread the sesame seeds about ⅛" thick on a flat baking pan or pie dish and bake for 12–18 minutes at 300°F. Stir once or twice and remove from oven when lightly browned and toasted. Blend the toasted seeds ¼ cup at a time in the blender until ground fine. Place the seeds and all remaining ingredients in the blender and liquefy. Heat in a saucepan on medium-low heat, stirring frequently, until thickened and hot throughout. Serve on vegetables, grain, burgers, casseroles or pasta. Keeps 6–8 days refrigerated.

Tahini Sauce
(Serves 6–8)

1 small or medium onion,
  chopped
2–3 Tbsp. natural oil
1 cup water
1 cup sesame tahini
2–3 Tbsp. tamari soy sauce

3 tsp. finely grated ginger
1 Tbsp. maple syrup *or* other
  liquid sweetener
1 tsp. sea salt
Several dashes nutmeg
Cayenne pepper to taste

Sauté the onion in hot oil until tender. Add the remaining ingredients and simmer everything on low heat for about 30 minutes. Serve hot over steamed vegetables and grains.

Gado Gado Spicy* Peanut Sauce
(Serves 6)

2 Tbsp. natural oil
1 large onion, chopped small
2–4 cloves garlic, minced

2½–3 cups water
1 cup natural peanut butter
½–1 cup unsalted peanuts,
   raw or roasted

4–5 Tbsp. fresh lemon juice
2–4 tsp. peeled, grated
   ginger root
4 tsp. liquid sweetener
4 tsp. apple cider vinegar
1 Tbsp. tamari soy sauce
½–¾ tsp. sea salt
Cayenne pepper to taste*

Heat the oil and sauté the onions and garlic until slightly tender, about 2–3 minutes. Add all the remaining ingredients, mix thoroughly and simmer on the lowest possible heat for 30–35 minutes, stirring occasionally. Serve over a medley of whole grains, cooked vegetables, raw vegetables and/or tofu as desired. Keeps 6–8 days refrigerated.

    *The sauce can be mild or spicy depending on how much cayenne is used.

Spicy Nut Sauce
(Serves 6)

2 Tbsp. natural oil
1 large onion, chopped small
2–4 cloves garlic, minced

2½–3 cups water
1 cup sesame tahini *or*
  cashew, hazelnut (filbert)
  or almond butter
4–5 Tbsp. fresh lemon juice
2–3 tsp. peeled, grated
  ginger root

½–1 cup raw or roasted
  sunflower seeds, cashews,
  hazelnuts, almonds or
  other nuts (larger nuts
  should be chopped)
4 tsp. liquid sweetener
4 tsp. apple cider vinegar
1 Tbsp. tamari soy sauce
½–¾ tsp. sea salt
Cayenne pepper to taste

Follow the directions for **Gado Gado Spicy Peanut Sauce** (above).

Orange Yam Sauce
(Makes about 5 cups; serves 4–6)

7½–8 cups peeled, chopped
  yams (3–4 large yams)*
¾ cup milk substitute (nut
  milk is best)
1 Tbsp. tamari soy sauce
2–3 tsp. white onion put
  through a garlic press
1–1½ tsp. curry powder

½–¾ tsp. sea salt
Several dashes cayenne
  pepper, to taste
Optional: several dashes sea
  kelp
Optional: 2 tsp. grated
  orange rind

Steam the yams until tender. Use a food processor or masher to mix all the ingredients thoroughly until smooth. Reheat the sauce on low heat in a saucepan or double boiler if desired. Serve hot over vegetables or whole grains, or serve on pasta noodles. Keeps 3–5 days refrigerated.

*Buttercup or butternut squash may be used sometimes instead of yams.

Yam Sauce with Green Herbs
(Makes about 5 cups)

7½–8 cups peeled, chopped yams (3–4 large yams)

¾ cup milk substitute (nut milk is best)

½ cup finely chopped green onions, green part only

¼ cup finely chopped fresh parsley

1 Tbsp. tamari soy sauce

1 tsp. vegetable sea salt, or more to taste

⅛–¼ tsp. *each* basil and dill weed

Several dashes cayenne pepper, to taste

Optional: several dashes sea kelp

Follow the directions for **Orange Yam Sauce** (above).

Sweet Onion Sauce
(Serves 4–6)

4 cups finely chopped onion

1 Tbsp. natural oil

⅓–½ cup water *or* broth

2–4 Tbsp. tamari soy sauce*

Sauté the onion in the oil and water on high heat, stirring constantly, until tender. Add the tamari and liquid, turn the heat to medium-low and cover the pan. Simmer for 1 hour and serve hot or cold over whole grains and/or vegetables, or use as a bread spread, gravy or topping for loaves, casseroles or burgers. Keeps 7–10 days refrigerated.

*2–4 Tbsp. miso may be used instead of the tamari, but a few tablespoons of the water must be withheld and mixed with the miso at the *end*, after simmering the onions.

Tomato Sauce
(Serves 6)

1–2 Tbsp. natural oil
1 large onion, chopped small
2–4 cloves garlic, minced
1 cup mushrooms *or* 1 small
  eggplant, chopped
4–6 large tomatoes, chopped
  or 1 - 28 oz (796 mL) can
  tomatoes, cored and
  chopped
1 - 14 oz (398 mL) can
  tomato paste
1–1½ cups water
3 bay leaves

1–2 Tbsp. tamari soy sauce
2–3 tsp. liquid sweetener (to
  balance flavours)
3 tsp. parsley
1–1½ tsp. *each* basil and
  oregano
¾–1 tsp. sea salt
½ tsp. *each* marjoram, thyme
  and rosemary, crushed
¼ tsp. sea kelp
Several dashes cayenne
  pepper to taste

Heat the oil in a large pot or Dutch oven on medium-high heat. When the oil is hot, add the onion and garlic and sauté for 1–2 minutes. Then add the mushrooms or eggplant and sauté for another 2 minutes or until fairly tender. Add the tomatoes and cook for 15–20 minutes until they turn to liquid. Add all the remaining ingredients and simmer the sauce on very low heat for 40–60 minutes, covered, stirring occasionally. A little extra water may be added for thinner consistency. Correct the herbs and spices if desired. When the sauce is finished, remove the bay leaves.

Keeps 6–8 days refrigerated. The recipe can be doubled or tripled for larger batches. Be sure to use less sea salt when increasing recipe sizes. Freezes well.

Mock Tomato Sauce
(Serves 6)

7 cups peeled, chopped orange yams *or* peeled butternut or buttercup squash

1 cup chopped fresh beets (about 2 medium)

1 cup chopped white or yellow onion

2 cloves garlic, minced

2–3 tsp. natural oil *or* 2–3 Tbsp. water

6 cups water *or* stock

2–3 Tbsp. tamari soy sauce

1 strip of wakame *or* kombu seaweed, washed and minced

3 tsp. parsley

1 tsp. basil

½ tsp. oregano

¼ tsp. *each* sea kelp, marjoram and thyme

⅛–¼ tsp. rosemary, crushed

1–2 bay leaves

2 tsp. liquid sweetener

2 tsp. apple cider vinegar

Steam the yams or squash and beets until tender. Sauté the onion and garlic in oil or water until transparent. Blend all the ingredients *except* the bay leaves until smooth, and heat in a saucepan with the bay leaves until hot throughout and the flavours mingle, 20 minutes or more. Remove the bay leaves and serve hot in place of spaghetti sauce or in lasagne, on pizza or over whole grains, vegetables, burgers or casseroles. Keeps 4–6 days refrigerated. May be frozen but is best fresh.

Avocado Tofu Sauce
(Serves 4–6)

14–16 oz (400–450 g) soft or regular tofu

2 medium or large ripe avocados, peeled and pitted

¼–½ cup water *or* stock

1–2 tsp. tamari soy sauce *or* miso

1 vegetable bouillon cube

Few dashes *each* cayenne pepper and sea kelp

Vegetable sea salt to taste

Use a food processor or homogenizing juicer to mix everything thoroughly. Heat on very low heat, stirring frequently, just until hot. Serve hot over vegetables, legumes, pasta or whole grains. Add a bit of lemon or pineapple juice if desired. Keeps 1–2 days refrigerated.

Garlic Sauce
(Serves 4–6)

1 cup water *or* stock

½ cup natural oil

8–10 cloves garlic, pressed

1–2 Tbsp. tamari soy sauce

1 tsp. paprika

½ tsp. *each* basil and thyme

¼–½ tsp. sea salt

Several dashes *each* cayenne pepper and sea kelp

Optional: 1–2 tsp. parsley

Beat the ingredients together with a wire whisk in a saucepan. Bring to a low boil on medium heat, stirring frequently. Then cover, turn down to low and simmer for 15–20 minutes until the flavours mingle and the sharp edge is off the garlic. Stir and serve. Keeps 1–2 weeks refrigerated.

Creamy Garlic Sauce

Grind 5 Tbsp. raw cashew pieces or blanched almonds to make 4 Tbsp. ground nuts. Use a blender to mix the ground nuts with all the ingredients in the **Garlic Sauce** (above), either before or after heating, to make a smoother, creamier garlic sauce with added flavour. Follow the directions for **Garlic Sauce**.

Basic White Sauce
(Serves 3–4)

1 cup thick nut milk *or* seed milk	2 tsp. natural light oil
1–2 Tbsp. unbleached white, kamut or rice flour	Several dashes cayenne pepper and sea salt to taste
1 Tbsp. arrowroot powder	*Optional:* 1–2 tsp. sweetener

Beat all ingredients together with a wire whisk. Stir the mixture over medium-high heat until it thickens to the desired consistency. Remove from heat at once to prevent further thickening. Serve hot.

Try the following variations and create your own new ones. Serve the sauce fresh and hot over steamed or baked vegetables, vegetable-grain dishes or pasta. Delicious, because you make it just the way you like it. The basic sauce keeps 2–4 days refrigerated.

White Sauce Variations

1. Add 1–2 tsp. dried parsley *or* 1–2 Tbsp. chopped fresh parsley or cilantro.

2. Add ½–1 tsp. dill weed or paprika.

3. Add extra cayenne pepper and several dashes ground cumin and coriander along with ½–1 tsp. curry powder. Turmeric is optional.

4. Add ½ cup sautéed sliced mushrooms or sautéed chopped onions.

5. Add ¼–½ cup chopped chives or chopped green onion tops.

6. Add ¼–⅓ cup cashew or blanched almond butter or nut pieces.

7. Blend all ingredients with 4 oz (120 g) regular tofu before heating. Add extra spices to taste.

8. Add 2 Tbsp. sesame tahini.

9. Add ½ cup chopped, steamed carrots to the mixture before blending.

10. Blend or mash ½–1 avocado thoroughly and mix it in *after* the sauce is heated. This makes a tasty, lovely green sauce, good hot or cold. If desired, sprinkle on a little chopped fresh parsley for extra eye appeal.

Arrowroot Sauce
(Serves 4–6)

2 Tbsp. arrowroot powder
1½ cups cool water
2–3 Tbsp. tamari soy sauce
1–2 vegetable bouillon cubes
 or 1–2 tsp. vegetable broth
 powder

Several dashes *each* cayenne
 pepper and sea kelp
Optional: Dash of sweetener
 (to balance flavours)

Mix the arrowroot thoroughly with the water in a saucepan, using a wire whisk. Add the remaining ingredients and mix well. Cook over medium heat, stirring constantly, until thickened. Keep warm over low heat. Serve over hot vegetables, whole grains or stir-frys. Keeps up to 7 days in the refrigerator, or may be frozen.

Vegan Pesto
(Serves 6)

3 large bunches fresh basil
 leaves (3 packed cups),
 stems removed
½ cup pine nuts
⅔ cup finely chopped fresh
 parsley
½–⅔ cup olive oil *or* ½ cup
 natural oil and 2 tsp.
 toasted sesame oil

6 Tbsp. engevita yeast *or*
 other yellow nutritional
 yeast
3–4 large cloves garlic,
 lightly chopped
½–¾ tsp. sea salt
Optional: 4 Tbsp. extra pine
 nuts

Combine all ingredients *except* the extra pine nuts in a food processor. Grind thoroughly until rather smooth. Add the extra whole pine nuts and grind a little more, or leave them whole. Serve with hot, drained pasta. Toss gently and serve with garlic bread, sliced red bell peppers, extra parsley and/or chopped green onion tops. Keeps 3–5 days refrigerated.

Easy Pesto Sauce
(Serves 4–6)

2–3 bunches fresh basil
    leaves
Handful of pine nuts,
    almonds, hazelnuts
    (filberts) *or* pecans

Olive oil
Garlic
Sea salt

In a blender, combine the basil leaves, nuts and enough olive oil to make the blades turn properly. Stop the blender occasionally to stir, then blend again. Add garlic and sea salt to taste. Blend until a smooth paste is formed. Serve tossed with hot pasta (or with vegetables!). Keeps 2–5 days refrigerated.

Kind-of-a-Pesto
(Makes 3½–4 cups; serves 8–10)

4 medium, ripe tomatoes
    (peeling optional) *or* 1 - 28
    oz (796 mL) can
    tomatoes, cored
1 small bunch spinach (1
    cup packed)
½ cup chopped green onion
    tops
½ cup finely chopped fresh
    parsley

½ cup olive oil *or* ½ cup
    natural oil and 2 tsp.
    toasted sesame oil
3–4 large cloves garlic,
    lightly chopped
4–5 tsp. basil
Sea salt or vegetable sea salt
    to taste
Optional: ⅓–½ cup engevita
    yeast *or* other yellow
    nutritional yeast
Optional: handful of raw nuts

Use a food processor to purée all the ingredients until smooth. Heat the pesto on medium-low heat until hot throughout. Serve over hot pasta, cauliflower, potatoes, turnips or whole grains. Keeps 5–7 days refrigerated.

Mock Cheese Sauce with Nutritional Yeast

½ cup engevita yeast *or* other yellow nutritional yeast

3 Tbsp. flour (whole wheat, kamut, brown rice, millet or quinoa)

4 tsp. arrowroot powder

½ tsp. sea salt

1 cup water

1 Tbsp. natural oil

Optional: 1–2 tsp. prepared Dijon or yellow mustard *or* ½–1 tsp. dry mustard

Mix the first four ingredients together, then add the water and oil and mix thoroughly with a wire whisk. Stir or whisk over medium to medium-high heat until the mixture thickens and begins to bubble slightly. Stir in the mustard, heat another 30–60 seconds and serve instead of cheese sauce over vegetables and/or whole grains.

Main Dishes

For preparation of main dish whole grains or legumes, see the **Special Foods** chapter.

Spelt Vegetable Burgers
(Serves 8)

½ cup parsnips *or* small turnips, chopped small

½ cup green pepper, chopped small

½ cup mushrooms, chopped small

1½ cups spelt flour

1 cup ground sunflower seeds *or* nuts (**Home Roasted** are best)

2 Tbsp. arrowroot powder *or* soy flour

½–¾ cup onion, chopped fine

1–2 cloves garlic, minced

½ cup water

3–4 Tbsp. olive oil

3 tsp. dried parsley *or* 3 Tbsp. finely chopped fresh parsley

½ tsp. *each* sea salt, basil, oregano and dill weed

Optional: 2–4 tsp. tamari soy sauce

Steam the vegetables (except for the onions and garlic—leave these raw) until tender, then mash them and add them to the remaining ingredients. Use a fork to mix well. Oil a frying pan or flat grill. Form the mixture into 8–12 burgers and lightly coat each one with extra flour. Cook them on medium-low heat for several minutes on each side until nicely browned and serve with mustard, Natural Ketchup or Tomato Sauce and a bun if desired.

Kamut Nut Burgers
(Serves 8)

2/3 cup carrots, chopped small

2/3 cup celery, chopped small

1⅓ cups flour: kamut, whole wheat, spelt or amaranth

1 cup ground nuts or seeds (almonds, hazelnuts [filberts] or sunflower seeds are best)

2 Tbsp. arrowroot powder *or* soy flour

½–¾ cup finely chopped onion

½ cup water *or* milk substitute

3–4 Tbsp. natural oil

3 tsp. parsley

½ tsp. *each*: sea salt, basil, oregano and thyme

Optional: 2–4 tsp. tamari soy sauce

Steam the carrots and celery until tender, then mash them and add all the remaining ingredients. Use a fork to mix well. Oil a frying pan or flat grill and cook on medium-low heat. Form the mixture into 8–12 burgers and lightly coat each one with extra flour. Cook them for several minutes on each side until nicely browned and serve with mustard, **Natural Ketchup**, gravy or BBQ sauce and a bun if desired.

Oat Nut Burgers
(Serves 8)

⅔ cup carrots, chopped small

⅔ cup celery, chopped small

1 cup rolled oats, ground in blender or food processor

½ cup rolled oats (whole)

1 cup ground nuts or seeds (almonds, hazelnuts [filberts] or sunflower seeds are best; also try pumpkin and sesame seeds)

1 tsp. baking soda *or* arrowroot powder

½–¾ cup finely chopped onion

½ cup water *or* milk substitute

3–4 Tbsp. natural oil

3 tsp. parsley

½ tsp. *each* sea salt, basil, oregano and thyme

Optional: 2–4 tsp. tamari soy sauce

Follow the directions for **Kamut Nut Burgers** (above).

Lentil Burgers
(Serves 6)

2 cups dry brown lentils, cooked until tender and drained

¾ cup bread crumbs *or* cracker crumbs

1 cup finely diced onion

2 Tbsp. arrowroot powder *or* unbleached white or kamut flour

2 Tbsp. miso *or* tamari soy sauce, *or* 2 vegetable bouillon cubes

3 tsp. parsley

1 tsp. dill weed

½ tsp. vegetable sea salt

Several dashes *each* cayenne pepper and sea kelp

Tomato juice

Optional: ½–1 cup chopped celery

Mix the warm lentils with all the other ingredients, using just enough tomato juice to hold the mixture together and shape into burgers. Add extra flour if needed. Heat an oiled frying pan or griddle to medium-hot. Cook burgers about 12–18 minutes on the first side and 6–12 minutes on the second side, or until nicely browned and warm throughout. These are best served without a bun, with **Natural Ketchup, Arrowroot Sauce, Tomato Sauce, Mushroom Gravy** or **Vegetarian Gravy**.

Wonderful Millet Vegetable Balls
(Serves 3–4; makes about 5 cups)

2 cups cooked millet, cold (about ¾ cup uncooked millet)

½ cup hazelnut (filbert) flour *or* ground almonds or other nuts

2 Tbsp. arrowroot powder *or* unbleached white or kamut flour

2–3 Tbsp. natural oil

1 cup chopped onion

1 cup broccoli *or* asparagus, chopped small

1 cup carrots, chopped small

1–1½ cups chopped mushrooms

1 cup celery *or* bell peppers, chopped small

½ cup chopped black or green olives

2 cloves garlic, minced

2 vegetable bouillon cubes

2–3 tsp. tamari soy sauce *or* miso

3–4 tsp. dried parsley *or* 2–3 Tbsp. chopped fresh parsley

1 tsp. dill weed

1 tsp. paprika

½ tsp. marjoram

½ tsp. thyme

Optional: ¼–½ tsp. sea salt (especially if unsalted bouillon cubes are used)

Optional: ½ cup **Home Roasted Almonds** or other nuts, chopped

Mix the first three ingredients separately. Heat the oil and sauté the onions, broccoli and carrots until semi-tender. Add the other vegetables and sauté 1–2 minutes more. Add all the remaining ingredients and sauté 1–2 minutes more. Break up the bouillon cubes in the stir-fry and mix them well with everything else. Remove the sauté from the heat and mix it well with the millet-flour mixture. Roll it into balls, using ⅛–¼ cup for each ball. Bake the balls at 400°F for 18–22 minutes until hot and toasted for a wonderful flavour, and serve with **Arrowroot Sauce**, **Mushroom Gravy**, **Vegetarian Gravy**, or **Toasted Cashew or Sesame Sauce**. Incredibly delicious!

The ⅛-cup balls may be stir-fried in a lightly oiled frying pan and served as "meat balls" with spaghetti and tomato sauce, or they can be eaten plain or served as suggested above. Cold leftover balls keep 4–6 days refrigerated. They are terrific for lunches and snacks—a wonderful protein and vitamin lift. Makes 2–4 dozen.

Rice or Quinoa Vegetable Balls

Instead of millet, brown rice may be used in the **Wonderful Millet Vegetable Balls** (above). Cook ⅞ cup of rice in 2¼ cups water so the rice is very tender. For Quinoa (*KEEN-wah*) Vegetable Balls, cook 1⅛ cups quinoa in only 2 cups water so the grain will be less tender than usual. Measure 2 cups of the cold cooked grain before using in the recipe.

Other grains may also be used. Experiment with kasha, buckwheat, pot barley, bulgur and other whole grains.

Millet, Rice or Quinoa Vegetable Burgers

Prepare the **Wonderful Millet Vegetable Balls** (above) and use ½–¾ cup of the mixture for each burger. Lightly coat the burger with whole wheat, kamut or spelt flour. Grill them for 4–5 minutes on each side on medium-high heat in a skillet or on a griddle. Serve with **Natural Ketchup**, mustard, pickle and a bun if desired.

Tofu Vegetable Balls or Burgers

Prepare the **Wonderful Millet Vegetable Balls** (above), except use 1 lb (450 g) of regular tofu, crumbled, instead of the millet.

T.V.P. Vegetable Balls or Burgers

Prepare the **Wonderful Millet Vegetable Balls** (above), but in place of the millet use 1 cup texturized vegetable protein (T.V.P. or texturized soy protein) soaked in ⅞ cup boiling water for 10 minutes or more until the T.V.P. expands and softens.

Tofu "Meat Loaf"

The dictionary defines *meat* as ". . . an edible portion of something: as coconut meat; food in general or anything eaten as nourishment," therefore meat need not refer to animal flesh.

Prepare the **Wonderful Millet Vegetable Balls** (above), except use 16 oz (450 g) regular tofu, crumbled, instead of the millet. Generously oil a large loaf pan or small square casserole. Line the bottom of the pan with wax paper and oil it again. Gently press the mixture into the pan and press sesame or sunflower seeds into the top, if desired. Bake at 375°F for 45–55 minutes until nicely browned and firm. Cool 5–10 minutes before slicing. Serve with your favourite sauce.

Savoury Bean Balls or Burgers
(Serves 4)

1 cup cooked beans, well drained and mashed (chick peas, pinto, adzuki or kidney beans are best)

2 cups steamed vegetables, chopped small (carrots, broccoli, celery, bell peppers, peas, asparagus, zucchini, etc.)

1 cup whole wheat or kamut flour *or* bread or cracker crumbs

½ cup finely diced onion

2 cloves garlic, pressed

2 Tbsp. nut butter (almond, cashew, sunflower, peanut or sesame butter, or sesame tahini)

1–2 Tbsp. miso *or* tamari soy sauce

3 tsp. parsley

1 tsp. paprika

½ tsp. *each* sea salt, basil, marjoram and thyme

Several dashes *each* cayenne pepper and sea kelp

Preheat the oven to 400°F. Mix all the ingredients together well. Add a bit of extra flour or water if desired to create the exact consistency you desire. Roll into balls, using ⅛–¼ cup of the mixture for each one. Bake for about 20 minutes or until browned and somewhat firm; or brown small balls 8–10 minutes in an oiled skillet on medium heat. Serve with a favourite sauce if desired. For burgers, use ⅔–¾ cup of the mixture for each burger, shape and flatten, and lightly coat each one in flour. Grill the burgers on medium-high heat for 4–5 minutes on each side. Serve with a bun, **Natural Ketchup** and all the fixings as you like, or top with a sauce or gravy. Keeps 4–7 days refrigerated and may be frozen.

Quick and Tasty Bean Balls or Pâté
(Serves 2–4)

1 cup cooked beans, well drained and mashed (chick peas, pinto, adzuki or kidney beans are best)

1 cup finely chopped steamed vegetables

2 Tbsp. sesame tahini

2 Tbsp. toasted sesame seeds *or* toasted sunflower seeds, ground

3–4 tsp. finely chopped fresh parsley

3 tsp. tamari soy sauce *or* miso

1 tsp. *each* vegetable sea salt, onion powder, garlic powder and paprika

½ tsp. *each* basil and cumin

¼ tsp. cayenne pepper

Several dashes sea kelp

Optional: 2 Tbsp. arrowroot powder *or* unbleached white flour

Optional: extra toasted, ground seeds

Mash all ingredients together thoroughly, and shape them into balls of any size. No extra cooking is required. Use the arrowroot or flour if needed to help keep the balls firm, or shape into a small loaf and slice. Use other favourite seasonings if desired. Chill before serving to stiffen but serve at room temperature for the best flavour. The balls may also be coated with extra ground, toasted sesame or sunflower seeds. This is a great recipe for using up leftover beans and vegetables! Try the balls hot, too: follow the cooking directions for the **Savoury Bean Balls or Burgers** (above).

Pot Luck "Meat" Loaf, Balls or Burgers

Use leftover whole grains, beans or steamed vegetables in any of the above recipes for balls, burgers or "meat" loaf. Exchange equal amounts of leftovers for similar ingredients called for in the recipes to create your own wonderful and unique taste creations.

Easy Tamari Tofu Sauté
(Serves 2)

8 oz (225 g) regular tofu
2–3 Tbsp. tamari soy sauce

Optional: several dashes cayenne pepper

Rinse the tofu and cut into french fry size strips or ½" square chunks. Put the tamari in a frying pan and heat on high heat. When the tamari starts to sizzle, add the tofu chunks and stir constantly over high heat for several minutes until most or all of the tamari is absorbed into the tofu and the tofu has a rich, brown seared coating. Serve at once as a side or main dish, by itself or with an added sauce like **Mushroom Gravy, Orange Yam Sauce, Creamy Cashew Sauce, Sweet Onion Sauce** or another favourite sauce of your choice. The tofu also tastes delicious all by itself, as the sauté process adds exceptional flavour.

Note: The pan will look hard to clean but wipes clean if soaked in water a few minutes.

Main Dishes

Marinated Broiled Tofu Strips
(Serves 4–6)

14–16 oz (400–450 g)
  regular tofu
Marinade:
1½–2 cups water
¼–⅓ cup tamari soy sauce,
  Quick Sip® *or* teriyaki
  sauce

½ tsp. *each* onion powder,
  garlic powder and curry
  powder
¼ tsp. *each* cumin and
  paprika
Several dashes *each* cayenne
  pepper and sea kelp

Freeze the block of tofu in its package or a plastic bag, overnight or until it is frozen solid. Defrost it by putting the package in hot water. When it is defrosted, remove the package, rinse the tofu and gently press out all the excess water. Slice the tofu into slabs about ½" thick.

    Simmer the tofu slices, covered, in the marinade for 15–20 minutes on medium-low heat. Then drain the tofu slices and broil them for 2–3 minutes on each side before serving plain, or with a sauce or gravy of your choice. Try **Vegetarian Gravy**, **Mushroom Gravy** or one of the nut sauces for the best flavour.

Tofu Rarebit
(Serves 4)

14–16 oz (400–450 g)
  regular tofu
2 cups **Tomato Sauce, Mock
  Tomato Sauce** *or*
  Mushroom Gravy
1–2 tsp. tamari soy sauce *or*
  miso *or* 1 vegetable
  bouillon cube
½ tsp. sea salt
½ tsp. paprika
Several dashes cayenne
  pepper

2–3 Tbsp. natural oil

1 small onion, chopped
2–3 stalks celery *or* green
  pepper, chopped
1–2 cups mushrooms, sliced
Optional: 10–14 black or
  green olives

4–8 slices whole grain toast
Garnishes: ½ cup or more
  chopped fresh parsley,
  tomato and/or avocado
  wedges, extra olives
  and/or other chopped
  fresh vegetables

Blend the tofu, sauce and all the seasonings until fairly smooth. Heat the mixture on medium-low heat until bubbling hot. While the sauce is heating, prepare the sautéed vegetables and toast. Heat the oil and sauté the onion and celery or green pepper until semi-tender. Then add the mushrooms and olives and continue to sauté until everything is as tender as you like it. Place the warm toast on a dinner plate, cover with the sauce and sautéed vegetables, and garnish as desired. Eat this dish with a knife and fork! The sauce and sautéed vegetables keep 2–3 days refrigerated.

Stir-Fried Vegetables with Horseradish on Whole Grains

Brown rice, millet, quinoa,
   buckwheat *or* kasha grain

3 Tbsp. toasted sesame oil
¼–½ cup sliced or chopped
   ginger root, peeled

Hard Vegetables:
2 carrots, sliced on a long
   diagonal about ⅛" thick
1 green pepper *or* 1 stalk
   broccoli, cut in long, thin
   pieces
2–4 stalks celery, sliced on a
   long diagonal about ⅓"
   thick
1–2 cups chopped bok choy
   or Chinese cabbage

Other Ingredients:
8–12 mushrooms, sliced
   (can be shitake or oyster)
½–1 cup mung bean sprouts
   or snow peas (deveined)
2–5 Tbsp. tamari soy sauce
1–2 Tbsp. grated ginger
2–5 tsp. prepared
   horseradish
Optional: 1 can water
   chestnuts, sliced
Optional: 4 oz (120 g) plain
   or marinated tofu, cut in
   small cubes
Optional: several dashes *each*
   cumin powder, coriander,
   cayenne pepper
Optional: ½ cup or more black
   bean sauce, bouillon broth
   or other Oriental sauce

Cook the whole grain until tender. While the grain is cooking, heat the oil in an Oriental wok, iron skillet or frying pan until hot and sizzling. Add the sliced ginger and sauté for 2–3 minutes, then add the hard vegetables and sauté another 3–6 minutes until fairly tender. Keep the heat just high enough so the vegetables keep sizzling the entire cooking time. Keep stirring.

   Add the remaining ingredients except for the sauce and sauté a few more minutes. (Some prefer to remove or avoid eating the ginger pieces after cooking their flavour into the dish.) Serve hot and enjoy over fresh, cooked whole grains. The vegetables keep 1–2 days refrigerated.

Stir-Fried Vegetables with Onions and Garlic on Whole Grains

Follow the directions for **Stir-Fried Vegetables with Horseradish on Whole Grains** (above), but omit the horseradish. Instead, sauté 1 medium or large white or yellow onion, chopped, along with 2–4 cloves chopped garlic with the ginger in the hot skillet before adding the hard vegetables.

Celebration Cabbage Rolls
(Serves 4–6)

2 cups kasha *or* buckwheat
1 medium onion, chopped
2 Tbsp. natural oil
3 cups (about ½ lb/250 g) mushrooms, sliced
2–4 Tbsp. sunflower seeds *or* chopped nuts, toasted
2 tsp. chopped fresh parsley
1 tsp. sea salt
½ tsp. *each* basil, paprika and dill weed

¼ tsp. sea kelp
⅛ tsp. or less *each* marjoram and savory
Several dashes cayenne pepper
10–16 large cabbage leaves, whole

2–3 cups **Tomato Sauce** or **Mock Tomato Sauce**, heated in a saucepan

Cook the grain until tender. In a large frying pan, sauté the onion in the oil until semi-tender for about 2 minutes. Add the mushrooms, nuts, herbs and spices and sauté for another 5 minutes or so until the onions are tender and transparent.

While the other ingredients are cooking, steam the separate cabbage leaves for 5 minutes or more until they are slightly tender but still a little crisp.

When the grains are finished cooking and the vegetables are sautéed, mix them all together. Fill each cabbage leaf with a little of the grain and vegetable mixture while everything is still hot. Fold up the cabbage leaves and tuck them, folded side down, in a large, shallow, lightly oiled baking dish. (A 9"x13" glass pan with 1–1½" sides works best.) If the leaves won't stay folded, use toothpicks to keep them in place. Be careful to count the toothpicks and remove them all before serving the cabbage rolls.

Cover the cabbage rolls with hot **Tomato Sauce** or **Mock Tomato Sauce** and bake them at 325°–350°F for 15–20 minutes until everything is totally hot and the sauce flavours the cabbage. Serve them immediately, using extra sauce from the bottom of the baking pan as gravy.

Kasha Pilaf

Follow the directions for **Celebration Cabbage Rolls** (above), but omit the cabbage and sauce. Use kasha grain cooked and sautéed with all the other vegetables and ingredients. Serve by itself or with a brown sauce or gravy.

Parsley and Rice Casserole
(Serves 4–6)

8 cups cooked brown rice
(about 2–2½ cups dry
with extra water)
2 Tbsp. natural oil
1 small or medium onion,
chopped small
2–3 cloves garlic, minced
Optional: 1–2 cups sliced
mushrooms
Optional: ½ cup pine nuts
2 vegetable bouillon cubes
½ cup water

¼ cup ground nuts
2 Tbsp. whole wheat, kamut
or spelt flour *or* arrowroot
powder
¾–1 cup dried parsley flakes
or 1–1½ cups finely
chopped fresh parsley
1 tsp. *each* dill weed, sea salt
and paprika
Optional: 1–2 tsp. tamari soy
sauce *or* miso

While the rice is cooking, sauté the onions and garlic in the hot oil until almost tender. Then add the mushrooms and pine nuts and sauté 1–2 minutes longer.

Preheat the oven to 350°F. Mix the hot rice with the bouillon cubes to soften them and combine thoroughly. Then add the sautéed mixture and all the remaining ingredients to the rice and mix carefully so as not to mash the rice. Place the mixture in a lightly oiled deep 9" or 10" baking dish and smooth the top. Sprinkle on extra paprika for added eye appeal. Bake for about 30 minutes until hot and somewhat firm throughout. Serve immediately. Keeps refrigerated for 5–7 days. Best if not frozen.

Spanish Vegetable Paella
(Serves 2–4)

1 cup dry brown rice *or* Basmati rice

Optional: 10–16 oz (350–450 g) marinated tofu (from **Marinated Broiled Tofu Strips**)*

2–4 Tbsp. olive oil

1 medium or large onion, chopped small

2–3 cloves garlic, minced

1 green pepper, chopped small

1 red bell pepper, chopped small

2 cups mushrooms, sliced

10–16 black or green olives, cut in half

½ small zucchini, quartered and chopped small

2 tomatoes, chopped small

2 vegetable bouillon cubes

¼ cup broth, tomato juice *or* water with tamari or miso added

½ tsp. powdered saffron or 1 g saffron strands

½ tsp. chopped fresh parsley

Sea salt and cayenne pepper to taste

Lemon wedges and parsley sprigs

Cook the rice and prepare the marinated tofu. In a large skillet or wok, heat the oil and sauté the onion and garlic until slightly tender. Then add all the vegetables except the tomatoes and sauté until the vegetables are tender but still a bit crispy or firm. Then add the tomatoes, bouillon cubes, liquid and spices and sauté 2–3 minutes more. Be sure to break up the cubes in the mixture. Then add the cooked rice and mix everything together for 30–60 seconds. Remove from the heat and keep covered for 2–5 minutes, then serve garnished with lemon wedges and parsley sprigs.

*Optional marinated tofu may be added with the rice.

Japanese Brown Rice Sushi

#1: Cook 1 cup dry, short grain brown rice and cool.
    or
#2: Cook 1 cup dry, short grain brown rice and cool. *Mix it with:*
2–3 Tbsp. rice vinegar and equal amount of:
2–3 Tbsp. barley malt powder or other natural granular sweetener
Sea salt, to taste

Choose 3 or more of the following for sushi filling:
Avocado, sliced
Pickled ginger
Cooked spinach leaves
Strips of raw leafy lettuce

Grated carrot
Strips of cucumber or zucchini
Plain or marinated tofu strips
Grated daikon radish
Lightly steamed asparagus
Green onion, tops only
Tender lotus root, cut in strips
Green or red bell pepper strips

Toasted (sushi) nori (seaweed sheets)
Wasabi powder (green horseradish), mixed with water to make paste
Liquid plum sauce

Place one sheet of sushi nori on a bamboo sushi mat with the bamboo in a horizontal position and the nori in the long, rectangular, horizontal position. Press ½" rice mixture onto the bottom two-thirds of the nori, ½" thick. Spread just a bit of the wasabi paste in a line across the middle of the rice and follow with plum sauce if desired. Place some fillings in a 1" thick strip, horizontally, in the middle of the rice. Lightly wet the top upper edge of uncovered nori like you would wet an envelope. Begin to roll up the bamboo and nori with fillings and let the uncovered nori roll up over the filled part. Use the mat to help you shape it into a perfect roll. The water will help seal it so it stays together. Use a sharp knife to cut off the rough ends of the roll and cut the roll in half in the middle. Then cut the two rolls each in half, then each in half one more time. Serve with extra pickled ginger, and wasabi and tamari soy sauce mixed together in a little dish for dipping the sushi in. Enjoy this easy, delicious sushi with dozens of filling combinations. It makes a perfect appetizer, snack or light meal. Keeps several days refrigerated. Should not be frozen.

Zesty T.V.P. with Sauces
(Serves 2 or more)

1 cup T.V.P. (texturized vegetable or soy protein)
7/8 cup boiling water
One of the following sauces (or your favourite similar sauce):
Toasted Cashew Sauce
Vegetarian Gravy
Mock Cheese Sauce
Tomato Sauce
Orange Yam Sauce
Gado Gado Spicy Peanut Sauce
Toasted Sesame Sauce
Mushroom Gravy
Creamy Cashew Sauce
Mock Tomato Sauce
Sweet Onion Sauce
Spicy Nut Sauce
Optional: 1 cup cooked whole grain
Optional: 1–2 cups steamed vegetables

Soak the T.V.P. in the boiling water for 10 minutes or until the T.V.P. expands and softens. Mix the tender T.V.P. into the sauce and heat it until it is hot throughout. Serve it over whole grains or steamed or sautéed vegetables for a delicious treat and a nutritious meal. The T.V.P. adds quick, easy and inexpensive protein to meals. It tends to absorb the flavours of the surrounding sauces and enhance them, though it has no particular flavour of its own. Extra sea salt, tamari or cayenne pepper may be added if desired.

Tangy T.V.P. and Bean Chili
(Serves 6–8)

2½ cups dry kidney or pinto beans, soaked and cooked

2–3 Tbsp. natural oil
2 cups chopped onion (about 1 large)
4–6 cloves garlic, minced
Optional: 1–2 green peppers, chopped
4–5 large tomatoes *or* 1 - 28 oz (796 mL) can tomatoes, cored and chopped

1 cup T.V.P. (texturized vegetable or soy protein)
⅞ cup boiling water

12–13 oz (364–398 mL) tomato paste
2 tbsp. tamari soy sauce
3 tsp. chili powder
2–3 tsp. parsley
1–1½ tsp. sea salt
1 tsp. oregano
½ tsp. sea kelp
¼ tsp. cumin seeds *or* powder (cominos)
⅛ tsp. cayenne pepper, or to taste
Optional: 1 tsp. crushed dried red chili peppers *or* 1–2 fresh hot peppers, chopped

While the beans are cooking, heat the oil in a large pot and sauté the onions and garlic for 2–3 minutes until semi-tender. Add the green pepper and sauté another 1–2 minutes. Add the tomatoes and simmer on low heat for 10–15 minutes. Meanwhile, mix the T.V.P. with the boiling water and let it sit for 10 minutes as it expands and softens. Then add the T.V.P. and all the remaining ingredients *except* the beans, to the vegetables. Simmer the sauce on low heat, covered, for 35–50 minutes.

When the beans are ready, drain them and save the liquid. Mix the sauce and beans together and add enough of the reserved bean liquid to bring the chili to the desired consistency. (Save the rest of the bean juice for **Vegetarian Gravy**.) Cook the chili for 20–30 minutes. Serve with chunks of bread or cornbread along with guacamole and/or salsa. Keeps refrigerated for 7 days or may be frozen.

T.V.P. Vegetable Goulash
(Serves 12–14)

6 medium potatoes, cut in
  1" chunks
1–1½ lbs carrots (7–8
  medium), sliced in
  ⅓"–½" chunks
Optional: 6–10 Jerusalem
  artichokes
Optional: 1–2 cups chopped
  broccoli *or* cauliflower

2 cups T.V.P. (texturized
  vegetable or soy protein)
1¾ cups boiling water
½–1 lb mushrooms (2½–5
  cups), halved or quartered
8–10 stalks celery, cut in 1"
  chunks
3–4 medium onions,
  chopped

2–3 green peppers *or* 2 small
  zucchini, cut in chunks
1–2 cups fresh or frozen
  corn *and/or* peas
2–3 Tbsp. tamari soy sauce
1–2 Tbsp. vegetable broth
  powder
2–4 vegetable bouillon cubes
2–3 Tbsp. parsley
1½ tsp. sea salt
1 tsp. basil
½ tsp. *each* paprika and sea
  kelp
⅛ tsp. cayenne pepper, or
  less to taste
Optional: ⅛ tsp. *each* cumin
  powder and thyme

In a large pot, steam the hard vegetables (potatoes, carrots, artichokes, cauliflower, broccoli) for 10–15 minutes. While the vegetables are steaming, add the boiling water to the T.V.P. and let it soak for 10 minutes until it expands and becomes tender. Next drain the steamed vegetables and return them to the pot without the steamer. Then add the T.V.P. and all the remaining ingredients. Use as many mushrooms as you like. Simmer everything together on low to medium heat for 20–25 minutes until the flavours mingle. Correct the seasonings as desired. Serve hot with a crusty bread. Keeps about 7 days refrigerated and freezes well. Hearty and nutritious!

Lentil Vegetable Goulash

Follow the directions for the **T.V.P. Vegetable Goulash** (above), but cook 2½ cups of dry brown lentils and add that instead of the T.V.P. Use the smaller amounts of vegetable broth powder and bouillon cubes. Delicious and satisfying!

Italian-Style Beans
(Serves 8–10)

1 lb (about 2 cups) white pea beans, haricots or navy beans, soaked and cooked until tender

2–3 Tbsp. natural oil (olive is best)

1½–2 cups onion, chopped small

2–4 cloves garlic, minced

½ cup chopped sweet pickles

½ cup chopped green olives with pimento

2 cups tomatoes, chopped

1 cup celery *or* green pepper, chopped small

3 tsp. parsley

1½ tsp. sea salt

1 tsp. dill weed *or* oregano

½–1 tsp. vegetable broth powder

½ tsp. basil

¼ tsp. paprika

⅛ tsp. sea kelp

Several dashes cayenne pepper

While the beans are cooking, heat the oil and sauté the onions and garlic on high heat until semi-tender. Then add the pickles, olives, tomatoes, green vegetables and all the seasonings, and simmer on low heat for 15–20 minutes, stirring occasionally, until the flavours mingle.

Preheat the oven to 350°F. When the beans are tender, drain them completely and mix the hot beans with the vegetable sauce. Lightly oil 1 large or 2 small baking dishes and spread the bean mixture about 2–2½" thick. Bake for 35–45 minutes. Keeps 5–7 days refrigerated.

Vegetable Casserole Supreme
(Serves 4–6)

1 cup dry chick peas (*or* soybeans), soaked, cooked and mashed (makes 2½ cups)

2–3 Tbsp. natural oil

1 cup chopped onion (about 1 medium)

2 cloves garlic, minced

2½ cups grated carrot (4–5 medium)

1 green pepper, chopped small

1 cup broccoli *or* green beans, chopped small

6–8 cups chopped celery

1½ cups sliced mushrooms

1–1½ cups water *or* broth

2 Tbsp. tamari soy sauce

½ cup wheat germ *or* cornmeal

2 Tbsp. sesame seeds *or* chopped nuts (roasted are best)

2 vegetable bouillon cubes *or* 1 Tbsp. vegetable broth powder

1 Tbsp. parsley

1 tsp. *each* basil, paprika and thyme

½ tsp. sea salt

¼ tsp. sea kelp

Several dashes cayenne pepper

Topping: 1–2 cups vegan chow mein noodles *or* small croutons

Cook the chick peas and discard all but 2–3 cups of the cooking water for mashing with the chick peas while still hot.

In a large skillet or pot, sauté the onion and garlic in hot oil for a minute or two. Add the vegetables one by one, beginning with the carrots. Sauté until all the vegetables are slightly tender. Then mix the vegetables with the remaining ingredients, including the mashed chick peas. Preheat the oven to 350°F. Spread the mixture into a 9" square baking dish and top with the chow mein noodles or croutons, pressing them lightly into the top of the casserole. Bake for 35–45 minutes until browned and cooked throughout. Keeps 5–7 days refrigerated, and may be frozen.

Mushroom and Tomato Stuffed Peppers
(Serves 6–12)

1 cup brown rice *or* millet
1–2 Tbsp. natural oil
2 small or medium onions, chopped
½ lb (225 g) mushrooms, sliced
1 tsp. *each* sea salt and parsley
½ tsp. *each* basil, oregano, sea kelp and paprika

⅛ tsp. or less *each* marjoram, thyme and savoury
Optional: 2 Tbsp. sesame seeds *or* ground sunflower seeds
6 green or red bell peppers, cut in half lengthwise, seeds and core removed
1½ cups **Tomato Sauce***
1 tomato, chopped fine

Cook the rice or millet for 45–60 minutes until the grain is finished cooking and is fairly dry. Preheat the oven to 350°F. In a large skillet or pot, heat the oil and sauté the onions and mushrooms and all the herbs until they are slightly tender. Then mix the cooked grain and sautéed vegetables together with 2–3 Tbsp. of the tomato sauce and the chopped tomato. Place the raw green or red peppers cut side up in a large, shallow baking dish. Fill the pepper shells with the grain and vegetable mixture. Fill the bottom of the baking dish around the peppers with about ½" of water. Bake the peppers for 20–30 minutes until the grain is very lightly browned and the peppers are tender but still a bit crisp.

While the peppers are baking, heat the rest of the tomato sauce over low heat until hot. When the peppers are finished baking, spoon the sauce over each serving of peppers and enjoy. Keeps 2–3 days refrigerated. Best if not frozen.

*Other sauces may be used instead of the Tomato Sauce. Try **Vegetarian Gravy**, **Mushroom Gravy** or **Arrowroot Sauce.**

Bravo Burritos
(Serves 6–8)

2 cups dry pinto beans,
kidney beans or black
(turtle) beans, soaked
2 cups chopped onion
(about 1 very large)
2–3 Tbsp. tamari soy sauce
3 tsp. chili powder
1 tsp. sea salt
⅛ tsp. cayenne pepper, or
less to taste
Several dashes sea kelp

Optional: 1–2 tsp. liquid
sweetener
12 flour tortillas
Extras:
Guacamole
Chopped tomatoes and
lettuce
Salsa
Optional: 6–12 oz dairy- and
casein-free tofu cheese,
brick or mozzarella style,
grated

Cook the beans and add the onion during the last 20 minutes of their cooking time, or sauté the onion separately in a couple tablespoons of oil for added flavour. Drain the beans and save the cooking liquid. While the beans are still hot, mix in the seasonings and add sweetener to balance the flavours, if desired. Mash most of the beans with a masher, fork or food processor. Add a little of the reserved cooking liquid to bring the beans to a thick but very spreadable consistency. Leave some beans whole in the mixture, for varied texture. (Save extra liquid for soups and sauces. It may be frozen.)

Heat the tortillas for 10 seconds on each side on a hot, ungreased griddle or in a frying pan. Put a few spoons of beans in the lower centre of each tortilla, along with some tofu cheese if used, and fold in the sides. Roll up the burrito from the bottom and use a bit of water to seal up the edges.

*Serve the burritos with the suggested extras or, if preferred, top the burritos with salsa or **Tomato Sauce** and bake for 10–15 minutes in a 350°F oven. Enjoy hot or cold. Keeps 5–7 days refrigerated. The bean mixture may be frozen.

Savoury Sloppy Jo's
(Serves 8–12)

1 lb (2½–3 cups) soy grits
  (soybean bits) *or* ground
  soybeans or chick peas
1–2 Tbsp. natural oil
2 medium onions, chopped
2 green peppers, chopped
1 tomato, chopped fine
2 Tbsp. tamari soy sauce
3 tsp. chili powder
½–1 tsp. sea salt, or to taste

½ tsp. sea kelp
Several dashes *each* cayenne
  pepper and allspice
Optional: ¼ cup pickles,
  chopped fine

2–4 cups **Tomato Sauce** *or*
  Mock Tomato Sauce
Whole grain buns or bread

Use real soy grits if available (dry bits of chopped soybeans about ¹⁄₁₆"–⅛" in diameter). Some products labelled soy grits are granular and won't work in this recipe. If soy grits are not available, use a meat grinder or food processor to grind whole soybeans, or chick peas that have been soaked but not cooked.

Soak and cook the soy grits or ground beans until tender. In a large skillet or pot, heat the oil and sauté the onions until semi-tender, add the green peppers and tomato and sauté another minute or more until everything is somewhat tender. Drain the hot bean bits and add them to the sautéed vegetables along with the herbs, spices and tamari. Cook on medium-low heat for 5 minutes longer, stirring frequently. Then add the sauce and simmer everything on low heat, covered, for 30–50 minutes while the flavours mingle and develop. Serve ½ cup or more of the Sloppy Jo mixture on a bun or bread, and eat it carefully like a burger or with a knife and fork. Keeps 6–8 days refrigerated or may be frozen.

Savoury Sloppy Jo's with T.V.P.

Follow the directions for **Savoury Sloppy Jo's** (above), but instead of soy grits or chick peas, add 3 cups dry T.V.P. soaked in 2½ cups boiling water for 10 minutes or more until the T.V.P. expands and softens.

Molasses and Beans Hot Pot
(Serves 6–8)

2 cups dry pinto beans
¾–1 cup molasses *or* sorghum
¾ cup **Natural Ketchup**

2 large onions, chopped
3–4 Tbsp. tamari soy sauce
½ tsp. dry mustard
½–1 tsp. sea salt

Soak the beans and cook in water until they are very tender. Keep 1–2 cups cooking liquid with the beans and drain off any excess (freeze it for later use in **Vegetarian Gravy** or soup stock). Add the remaining ingredients and mix well. Simmer the mixture for 20–30 minutes over low to medium heat. Serve hot as a main or side dish, by itself or over rice or another whole grain. This dish is exceptionally high in iron and calcium.

Vegan Roast
(Serves 4–6)

2 cups cooked and mashed chick peas* (about ¾ cup dry)

Cut into ¼" pieces:

1½ cups (about 3–4 small) finely chopped carrots

1½ cups (about 2–3 stalks) finely chopped celery

1½ cups (about 2) finely chopped parsnips *or* small white turnips with ⅛ tsp. cinnamon added to the main mixture

2–3 vegetable bouillon cubes

2–3 Tbsp. tamari soy sauce

1 tsp. sea salt *or* vegetable sea salt

¼ tsp. sea kelp

⅛ tsp. or less cayenne pepper

2 cups (about 1 very large) finely chopped onion

6 cups bread cubes, cut in about ½" squares

2 cups chopped mushrooms

1½–2 cups partially ground nuts *or* seeds (raw pecans, almonds, filberts or sunflower seeds taste best)

¾–1 cup chopped fresh parsley

¾ cup buckwheat *or* amaranth flour

¼ cup arrowroot powder, soy flour *or* chick pea flour

Optional: 2–4 cloves garlic, pressed

Soak the chick peas overnight and cook until tender. Steam the carrots, celery and parsnips or turnips until tender. Mash the chick peas and vegetables with the bouillon and other flavourings until thoroughly mixed and smooth. Add the raw onion and all the remaining ingredients and use your hands to mix everything together well. Preheat the oven to 350°F. Oil a 9"x13" low baking dish and line it with wax paper, then oil the wax paper. Shape the mixture into a 3"-high, oblong loaf in the pan with rounded top and edges. Bake for 80–90 minutes until well browned and cooked as firmly as you like it. The roast easily removes from the wax paper and can be placed on a platter on a bed of greens and garnished with peeled tomato flowers or radish roses. A thin coating of flax seed oil or other fresh, natural oil may be brushed on top for a glistening finish to the loaf. Looks terrific and tastes delicious with **Vegetarian Gravy** or **Mushroom Gravy**. Keeps 5–7 days refrigerated, or may be frozen. A wonderful main dish for holiday meals and special occasions!

*Pinto, kidney or adzuki beans may be used instead of chick peas.

Spinach Tofu Calzones
(Serves 2–4)

Crust:
1½ tsp. baking yeast
⅔ cup very warm water
  (about 110°–115°F)
2 tsp. maple syrup *or* 3 tsp.
  other liquid sweetener
2–2¼ cups kamut flour *or*
  1–1¼ cups whole wheat
  flour and ¾–1 cup
  unbleached white flour or
  whole wheat pastry flour
½–¾ tsp. sea salt
2 tsp. natural oil
Extra flour

3 large bunches (or 4 small)
  fresh spinach, washed and
  lightly chopped
6–7 green onions, chopped
1 green pepper, chopped
  small
2½–3 cups mushrooms
  (about 18 medium), sliced
  thin

2 cloves garlic, minced
2 Tbsp. natural oil
8–10 oz (225–300 g) regular
  tofu, rinsed and crumbled
2–3 Tbsp. toasted sunflower
  seeds *or* other toasted
  chopped nuts
4–6 tsp. tamari soy sauce
2–3 Tbsp. chopped fresh
  parsley *or* 2–3 tsp. dried
  parsley flakes, crushed
1 tsp. *each* sea salt, curry
  powder and basil
¼ tsp. *each* marjoram, dill
  weed and thyme
1/16–⅛ tsp. cayenne pepper
Optional: 8 oz (225 g)
  dairy-free/casein-free soy
  cheese, mozzarella or
  brick style, grated

3–4 cups **Tomato Sauce** or
  Mock Tomato Sauce

Begin by making the crust. Stir the yeast into the warm water and let sit for a few minutes. Add the sweetener, mix well and let sit another few minutes. Add half the flour and all the remaining ingredients, *except* the oil and extra flour, and mix thoroughly with a fork. Slowly add the remaining flour and use your hands to mix once the mixture gets too stiff. Knead the dough for 5–10 minutes. Put the oil in a 2–3 qt bowl and spread it around. Place the dough in the bowl and press it into the oil, turning it over and coating the other side as well. Cover the bowl with wet paper towels or cloth and place the dough in a warm place to rise, about 1 hour until just about doubled.

While the crust is rising, steam the spinach until tender and chop the other vegetables. In a large skillet or pot, heat the oil. When it is hot, sauté the green onions, green pepper and mushrooms until tender. Add the seasonings along with the crumbled tofu during the last half of the sauté.

When the dough is ready, preheat the oven to 425°F. Knead down the dough a minute or so and divide it into four parts. Knead each part 1–2 minutes and form it into a ball. Roll out each ball into a circle about 7" in diameter, using extra flour if needed to keep it from sticking, and turning the circle upside down occasionally. Add the spinach and soy cheese to the vegetable-tofu mixture and put a quarter of the mixture on half of the rolled dough circle. Fold the circle in half. Turn up and press the edges together with a fork, all around, to create a half-moon turnover. Repeat the process with the other three calzones. Poke fork holes all over the top of each calzone and place them on a lightly oiled flat baking sheet. Bake 20–25 minutes until nicely browned and firm. Serve smothered in hot **Tomato Sauce** or **Mock Tomato Sauce** and enjoy with a leafy green salad. The calzones freeze well or can be refrigerated for several days.

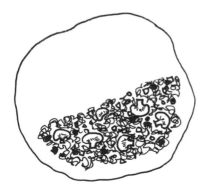
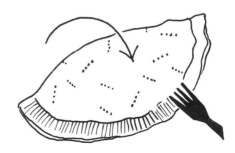

Fantastic Fondues

Choose 3–4 cups of the following per person:

Chunks of raw or steamed vegetables: tomatoes, carrots, celery, red or green bell peppers, zucchini, broccoli or cauliflower florets, parsnips, Brussels sprouts, etc.)

Plain or marinated tofu chunks

Bread chunks or cubes

Cooked **Wonderful Millet Vegetable Balls** or other whole grain, bean or tofu balls (make these extra firm so they hold together well)

Mochi (available at health food stores), cut into small squares and lightly pan-fried or baked, but still tender

One or more of the following sauces (depending on how many fondue pots you have):

Avocado Sauce
Toasted Cashew Sauce
Toasted Sesame Sauce
Vegetarian Gravy
Mock Cheese Sauce
Tomato Sauce
Mock Tomato Sauce
Orange Yam Sauce

Gado Gado Spicy Peanut Sauce
Creamy Garlic Sauce
Mushroom Gravy
Creamy Cashew Sauce
Sweet Onion Sauce
Spicy Nut Sauce

Heat the sauces on medium heat in a saucepot, then place them in the fondue pot(s) with the candle flames below. Dip the other ingredients into the sauces and enjoy. This is everything you need for a simple or elegant satisfying meal—a wonderful treat for family or entertaining guests. Fresh ingredients keep 1–2 days.

Pita Pizzas
(Serves 2–4)

2–3 cups **Tomato Sauce** *or* **Mock Tomato Sauce**
1–3 pita breads per person
8–12 oz (1–1½ cups) tofu cheese, grated (brick or mozzarella style without dairy or casein) *or* 6–8 oz (225 g) regular tofu, mashed, *or* **Easy Tofu Sauté**, mashed

Toppings: pineapple chunks, tomato slices, zucchini slices, green or red bell pepper strips, sliced olives, sliced mushrooms, spinach, pine nuts or other chopped nuts

Heat the tomato sauce while heating the broiler. Lightly toast the pita and spread on the hot tomato sauce. Sprinkle on tofu or tofu cheese and an assortment of toppings. Place the breads on a flat baking tray and broil for 1–4 minutes, until the cheese is melted and everything is hot and bubbly. The pitas keep 1–2 days refrigerated and they taste great cold for lunches, snacks or a whole light meal.

Pizza Breads
(Serves 2–4)

Follow the directions for **Pita Pizzas** (above), but substitute slices of whole grain bread or French bread, sliced as for submarine sandwiches, for the pitas.

Stuffed Canneloni or Conchiglie

1 batch **Scrambled Tofu**
¾–1 lb (335–450 g)
   canneloni *or* conchiglie
   (large pasta shells)
3–4 cups **Tomato Sauce** *or*
Mock Tomato Sauce

Optional: 8–12 oz dairy- and
   casein-free soy cheese
   (brick or mozzarella style
   are best), grated, *or* ½
   batch **Mock Cheese Sauce**

Preheat the oven to 350°F. Prepare the ingredients for **Scrambled Tofu**. Cook the pasta in a large pot of boiling water for 7 minutes or more until tender or *al dente*. While the pasta is cooking, scramble the tofu. Stuff the shells with the tofu mixture and place them in a shallow glass or ceramic baking dish. Cover with the sauce and grated soy cheese and bake for 8–12 minutes until everything is hot and bubbly. Serve immediately and enjoy.

   *For a "cheesier" flavour, mix ½ batch **Mock Cheese Sauce** with the tofu before stuffing the pasta.

PASTA

Preparing Noodles

Bring a large pot of water to a boil. When it is bubbling hard, add the noodles. Most noodles expand to 2–3 times their size. Mung noodles expand to 6–8 times their size.

   After adding the noodles, wait for the water to boil again, then turn down the heat *but make sure the water keeps bubbling*. Salt and oil do not need to be added if these directions are followed. Be careful not to overcook, as some of these noodles will fall apart or get very mushy from overcooking.

   Some like to test noodles for doneness by throwing one of them against a wall—if it sticks, it is ready to eat. Or taste a noodle. When it is just a little chewy, yet tender, it is just right. This is called *al dente* in Italian. The noodles should not be mushy or too hard,

164

but the best rule is that they should be as soft or hard as you personally prefer them. Drain, rinse if desired and serve.

Serve noodles with your favourite sauce. Various approximate cooking times for each type of noodle are listed below, along with some basic brand names and sources to buy noodles. Remember that cooking times will always vary, depending on quantity of noodles, amount of cooking water, size and type of pot and other factors.

Serve the noodles with one of the **Pesto Sauces, Tomato Sauce** or any of the gravies, **Nut Sauces** or **Yam Sauces**. Types and cooking times for noodles follow, along with some popular brand names.

Brown Rice Noodles (Pastariso)

Spaghetti and a few other shapes of noodles are available. Cook in 8–11 minutes.

Buckwheat Noodles (Westbrae)

Flat spaghetti noodles. Cook in about 8 minutes.

Corn Noodles (De Boles)

Assorted noodles are available, from lasagne, macaroni elbows and bows to spaghetti. Various cooking times, depending on style of noodles. Check package for directions.

Kamut Noodles (Artesian Acres)

Spaghetti noodles. See package for directions.

Mung Noodles (Canasoy and Chinese stores)

In thread-like strands like angel hair. Cook in about 12 minutes.

Quinoa (*KEEN-wah*) Noodles
(Artesian Acres, Quinoa Corp.)

Assorted shapes available. See package for cooking times. Corn or whole wheat are added to some brands.

Rice Noodles
(Canasoy, Eden and Chinese stores)

Clear ribbon noodles. Cook in about 8–10 minutes.

Soy-Rice Noodles (Canasoy)

Available in macaroni elbows and sometimes in ribbons. Cook in 12–15 minutes.

Spelt Noodles (Del Bonita, Purity Foods)

Several shapes of noodles available. Cook in 10–12 minutes.

Whole Wheat Noodles
(Michelle's, Eden, Westbrae, Eddie's, Natur)

All kinds of noodles available, from lasagne to spaghetti with every shape and size in between. Some also come in vegetable flavours like carrot, spinach, asparagus, etc. Depending on the thickness and how heavy the whole wheat is, they take 4–15 minutes to cook! See package directions or test for doneness after 4 minutes.

Wild Rice Noodles (Northern Lights)

Come in spaghetti noodles and elbows, sometimes other shapes. Package says to cook 2–4 minutes, but I suggest 8–14 minutes.

Vegetables

Amazing Artichokes
(Serves 2)

2 globe artichokes

Dipping sauces: **Tofu Mayonnaise, Veggie Butter** or **Citrus Sauces**

The Art of Selection and Preparation

Choose firm, dark green (with no purple or "fuzz"), unwrinkled globe artichokes. Wash and cut off all the stalk except for about ¼". Pull off and discard the first row of leaves around the stalk. With a sharp, serrated knife, trim ¾–1" from the tip of the artichoke and discard. Snip ¼–½" off the tip of each remaining leaf with a scissors or knife. Place the vegetables upside down (top down, stalk up) in a vegetable steamer over mildly boiling water and steam for 40–50 minutes until very tender. When a knife slides in and out easily, it is done.

Serve with one of the suggested dipping sauces.

How to Eat an Artichoke

Starting with the bottom row of leaves nearest the stalk, pull off one leaf at a time and dip the part that was attached to the artichoke in the sauce. With the inner part of the leaf facing

167

upwards, pull the base of the leaf between your teeth, pulling off all tender, easy-to-chew parts. (These are the edible parts.) Discard the rest of each leaf. As you get closer to the centre, you can eat more of each leaf as they get more tender. When you reach the "choke," scrape off the stringy, prickly part and discard. What's left is *entirely* edible! Dip it in the sauce and enjoy the best part—the heart, a delectable treat. Savour the delicious, stimulating aftertaste of the artichoke in your mouth—absolutely sensuous! If possible, share the experience with a loved one. Artichokes are another specialty for the liver.

Beet Treat
(Serves 2)

1–3 fresh beets, grated   Juice of 1–2 fresh lemons

Mix the beets and lemon juice together and serve on lettuce or spinach leaves, or in or around an avocado half. Delicious! The lemon juice makes the beets taste sweet and the beets are a wonderful treat for the liver. Do not use storage beets!

Baked Potato or Turnip Fries
(Serves 4)

6–8 medium white potatoes   Natural oil
  or small white turnips,   Sea salt
  peeled or unpeeled

Preheat the oven to 350°–375°F. Chop the vegetables into french fry size strips and use a brush to coat lightly with oil. Place on an oiled flat baking sheet and salt lightly if desired. Bake for 20 minutes or more until the fries are very tender. Serve hot and enjoy.

Baked Turnips*
(Serves 2)

2–3 fresh, small purple and white turnips

Preheat the oven to 400°F. Choose firm, bright-coloured, purple and white turnips. Scrub them with a good scrub brush and cut off the tip root and the stem end. Slice in ¼" rounds and place about ¼" apart on a lightly oiled baking sheet. Bake for 9–14 minutes until very tender, but not dry. Delicious plain, or try the variations below.

*Yams, winter squash chunks or sweet potatoes may be substituted for turnips.

Herb-Baked Turnips
(Serves 2–3)

¼ cup natural oil	Few dashes *each* cayenne
1 tsp. dried parsley, crushed	pepper and sea kelp
½ tsp. dried basil, crushed	3–4 medium turnips,
⅛–¼ tsp. sea salt	unpeeled, sliced ¼" thick

Mix all the ingredients together well *except* the turnips. Dip the turnip slices in the mixture and follow the directions for **Baked Turnips** (above).

Glazed Turnips
(Serves 2–3)

¼–⅓ cup maple syrup	Couple dashes sea kelp
2–3 Tbsp. natural oil	3–4 medium turnips,
Several dashes sea salt	unpeeled, sliced ¼" thick

Mix the maple syrup thoroughly with the oil and seasonings. Dip the turnip slices in the mixture and follow the directions for **Baked Turnips** (above).

Mashed Yams or Squash
(Serves 4)

2–4 medium yams *or* pieces
   of winter squash

Steam the yams or the cut squash pieces until tender. (You may bake them instead.) Peel or leave the skins on. Mash the very tender vegetables with a small-holed hand masher or, if skins are left on, use a food grinder or processor to blend in the skins. Add a milk substitute and sea salt, cinnamon or other seasoning to add flavour. Whip the vegetables just like mashed potatoes and serve hot. Children especially love this easy-to-eat treat. Add a bit of maple syrup to create **Mapley Mashed Yams or Squash.**

Easy Cinnamon Baked Squash
(Serves 4)

1 medium or large butternut   water
   or buttercup squash   cinnamon

Cut the squash in half with a sharp knife from top to bottom. Scoop out and discard the seeds or save for roasting. Fill the hollowed portion of the squash with water and sprinkle the entire top of it with cinnamon. Place the squash halves in a low baking pan with ½"–¾" water in the pan. Bake at 400°F for 45–60 minutes or until a knife moves in and out easily and the squash is very tender. Cut and serve hot.

Quick Baked Winter Squash
(Serves 2)

1 medium or large butternut, buttercup, acorn or turban
  squash *or* 2 large pieces cut hubbard or other large squash

Preheat the oven to 400°F. Cut the squash in half and scoop out
the seeds or cut 2 single-size servings from a larger squash. Place
the pieces, cut side down, on a lightly oiled *flat* metal pan or sheet,
and bake for 25–40 minutes until tender and a knife passes
through it easily. This is one of the quickest ways to bake squash.

Spanish Mushrooms in Garlic Sauce
(Serves 4–8)

3–4 Tbsp. olive oil
5 cloves garlic, sliced
1 lb mushrooms (about
  4½–5 cups), sliced thick
2–3 Tbsp. tamari soy sauce

½ dried chili pepper, seeds
  removed, left in 1 piece
2–4 Tbsp. finely chopped
  fresh parsley

Heat the oil over medium heat and add the garlic. When the garlic
begins to brown, add the mushrooms and sauté until almost
tender. Add the tamari and chili pepper and sauté for 1–2 more
minutes. Remove the pepper, sprinkle with the parsley and serve
hot as a side dish, or with toothpicks as a party appetizer. These
are best if eaten fresh but may be stored in the refrigerator 1–2
days if needed.

Tangy Stuffed Tomatoes
(Serves 2–4)

4 medium or large ripe
   tomatoes

1 recipe for **Humus, Falafel**
   or **Mock Tofu Egg Salad**

Wash and core the tomatoes. Scoop out a third to a half of the insides of each tomato and save it for other recipes. Stuff the tomatoes with one of the fillings and serve as is for a great snack or small meal. For added flavour, broil for a few minutes and serve with a creamy sauce or dressing.

Broiled Tamari Vegetables
(Serves 4)

1 small zucchini, sliced in
   ⅓" thick rounds
1 green pepper, cut in
   chunks
1 large tomato, cut in chunks

12 small mushrooms, whole
Optional: ½–⅓ cup
   pineapple chunks
Tamari soy sauce

Arrange the vegetables artistically and closely in a 9"x9" or 10"x10" shallow ovenproof baking dish. Pour or brush on about ⅓–½ cup tamari mixed with ¼–½ cup water. Baste the vegetables if not using a brush. Broil 5–14 minutes, depending on your broiler, until the vegetables are nicely browned and very tender. Enjoy hot as a side dish or over cooked whole grains. Add tofu chunks for extra protein and other nutrients.

Marinated Vegetable Medley
(Serves 4 or more)

¼ cup natural oil
¼ cup flax seed oil *or*
  additional natural oil*
2½ Tbsp. apple cider vinegar
4 tsp. parsley flakes, crushed
2 tsp. tamari soy sauce
½–¾ tsp. sea salt
½ tsp. basil
½ tsp. oregano
Several dashes *each* sea kelp,
  vegetable sea salt and
  cayenne pepper

3–4 cups chopped vegetables,
  in 1" or smaller pieces,
  including one or more of
  the following:
Cucumber or zucchini,
  sliced or quartered
Tomato chunks
Mushroom chunks or slices
Small broccoli or cauliflower
  florets, raw or
  pre-steamed 3–5 minutes
Green, red, yellow or purple
  bell pepper chunks

Beat all the ingredients together *except* for the vegetables. Add the vegetables and toss the mixture to coat the vegetables in oil and herbs. Be sure to use only apple cider vinegar, as it helps tenderize the vegetables and adds the right flavour. Let sit in the refrigerator for 1–2 hours, tossing occasionally, until the flavours mingle and the vegetables soften. Then drain the vegetables and let them sit at room temperature for 5–8 minutes before serving. This way the flavours will be more distinct. Save the leftover oil and herb mixture to make a new batch within 2 days, or store any leftover marinated vegetables in this mixture to preserve them for up to 3 or 4 days in the refrigerator. Serve the vegetables by themselves with toothpicks as a party appetizer or snack. They also make a nice salad when served over an avocado half on a bed of spinach leaves or chopped lettuce.

  *Pumpkin oil may also be used. Raw pumpkin or flax oil adds essential Omega 3 and 6 and is beneficial for skin, hair and nails. According to some sources, pumpkin oil may provide beneficial nutrients for prostate problems.

Lemony Green Vegetables
(Serves 2–4)

2–4 cups artichoke hearts (packed in water), drained, *or* broccoli, asparagus, Brussels sprouts, kohlrabi, dark greens or zucchini

1 recipe **Citrus Sauce #2**

Steam the vegetables until tender and serve hot covered in hot **Citrus Sauce #2**. For extra tang, add 1–2 tsp. grated lemon or orange rind to the sauce while it cooks.

Garden Vegetables with Mock Cheese Sauce
(Serves 2–4)

2–4 cups chopped white or green vegetables: cauliflower, potatoes, green beans *or* other green vegetables (see suggestions in **Lemony Green Vegetables**, above)

1 recipe **Mock Cheese Sauce**

Steam or bake the vegetables until tender and serve hot covered in hot **Mock Cheese Sauce**. Garnish with chopped fresh parsley or chives.

Cakes, Frostings, Toppings

Fudgy Brownies

1 cup flour: whole wheat,
  kamut or amaranth
½ cup carob powder
⅓ cup unbleached white
  flour *or* arrowroot powder
1–1½ tsp. no-alum baking
  powder
½ tsp. sea salt

¾ cup maple syrup *or* fruit
  concentrate
¼ cup water *or* apple juice*
⅓ cup natural light oil
2 tsp. real vanilla
Optional: ½–1 cup chopped
  raw nuts

Mix the first five dry ingredients together well. In a separate bowl, mix the remaining wet ingredients thoroughly. Slowly beat the dry into the wet ingredients and fold in the nuts. Preheat the oven to 350°F. Lightly oil an 8"x8" or 9"x9" square baking pan and dust it with flour. Scoop in the batter, smooth the top and bake for 25–30 minutes. Don't overbake. The brownies should be moist and tender. Cool before removing from the pan. Add frosting if desired. Keeps 5–7 days refrigerated.

*Peach or pear juice may also be used.

"Chocolatey" Carob Cake
(Makes a 9"x13" cake or a 2-layer 8" or 9" cake)

Wet ingredients:
1–1½ cups maple syrup *or* fruit concentrate
¾–1½ cups thick **Nut Milk**
½ cup natural light oil
2 Tbsp. liquid lecithin *or* 4 Tbsp. flax gel
2 tsp. real vanilla extract
Optional: 1 Tbsp. finely grated orange or lemon rind

Dry ingredients:
1½ cups whole wheat, kamut *or* spelt flour
¾ cup unbleached white *or* whole wheat pastry flour
¼ cup arrowroot powder
⅔ cup carob powder (dark roasted or regular)
3 Tbsp. powdered egg replacer
3–4 tsp. baking powder
1 Tbsp. instant coffee substitute (for a chocolatey taste)
2 tsp. gluten flour *or* 1 tsp. guar gum or xanthan gum
½ tsp. sea salt
Optional: ¼–½ cup chopped pecans, walnuts, hazelnuts (filberts) *or* pine nuts
Optional: shredded unsweetened coconut

Preheat the oven to 325°F. Combine the wet ingredients, using just ¾ cup of nut milk to start, and mix well. In a separate bowl, sift together the dry ingredients, then add slowly to the wet ingredients, beating with a wire whisk or a mixer. The mixture should be thick but pourable, and taste too sweet (with liquid sweeteners, most of the sweetness cooks off). If it is too dry, gradually add the remaining nut milk as needed.

Beat the batter 150–200 strokes until smooth, then mix in the nuts. Lightly oil the cake pan(s), and dust lightly with flour. Pour in the cake batter and bake 50–65 minutes until the cake is lightly browned and a toothpick comes out clean. Cool the cake before removing from the pans and top with **Carob Fudge Topping**. Sprinkle coconut on top if desired. Keep refrigerated up to 1 week, or slices may be frozen.

Double Carob Cake

Follow the directions for **"Chocolatey" Carob Cake** (above), but add 1–2 cups carob chips to the batter with the nuts.

Poppyseed Cake
(Makes a 9"x13" cake or a 2-layer 8" or 9" cake)

1¼ cups water
6 Tbsp. ground cashews *or* blanched almonds, raw
1 cup poppy seeds
Wet ingredients:
½ cup natural light oil
1½ cups maple syrup
1 cup natural raw sugar, brown date sugar or other natural granular sweetener
4 tsp. liquid lecithin *or* 3–4 Tbsp. flax gel
2 Tbsp. lemon juice
2 tsp. lemon rind

Dry ingredients:
2 cups kamut flour *or* 1¼ cups whole wheat flour and ¾ cup unbleached white flour or whole wheat pastry flour
¼ cup soy milk powder
4 Tbsp. arrowroot powder *or* egg replacer
3½ tsp. no-alum baking powder
2 tsp. guar gum *or* gluten flour
¾–1 tsp. sea salt

Blend the water and ground nuts. Add the poppy seeds and heat the mixture on medium-low heat until it comes to a boil, then cover and set aside for 30 minutes. Mix the wet and dry ingredients separately. Add the poppyseed mixture to the wet ingredients, then add the dry and mix thoroughly. Taste the batter. It should taste overly sweet, as most of the sweet taste cooks off! Add more dry or wet sweetener if needed for flavour and keep the mixture thick but easily stirrable. Preheat the oven to 350°F. Beat the batter until smooth—at least 200 strokes. Bake in lightly oiled and floured pan(s) for 50–60 minutes until browned and firm. Cool and add chilled frosting. Refrigerate in between servings. Keeps 4–7 days.

Petey Pumpkin Cake
(Makes 1 - 9"x13" sheet cake or 1 - 8" 2-layer cake)

Wet ingredients:
1½–2 cups maple syrup *or* fruit concentrate
2 cups cooked, mashed pumpkin (see **Pumpkin for Recipes**)
¾ cup natural light oil
½ cup or more thick nut milk
2–4 Tbsp. Barbados molasses *or* sorghum
2 Tbsp. liquid lecithin *or* 4 Tbsp. flax gel
2 tsp. real vanilla

Dry ingredients:
1½ cups kamut flour or whole wheat flour *or* 1¾ cups spelt flour
1 cup unbleached white flour, whole wheat pastry flour *or* kamut flour
½ cup amaranth flour, buckwheat flour *or* soy flour
3 Tbsp. powdered egg replacer
2 Tbsp. arrowroot powder *or* 2 tsp. guar gum or xanthan gum
3–4 tsp. no-alum baking powder
2–3 tsp. cinnamon
¾–1 tsp. sea salt
Optional: 1–2 Tbsp. gluten flour (greatly improves rising)
Optional: ½ cup chopped raw nuts (fresh walnuts or pecans are best)
Optional: ½–1 cup raisins *or* currants

Preheat the oven to 350°F. Combine the wet ingredients. Sift the dry ingredients into a separate bowl. Slowly stir the dry into the wet ingredients and beat 200 strokes or 2–3 minutes with an electric mixer. Stir in the nuts. The mixture should be thick but pourable. Add extra flour or nut milk if necessary. Lightly oil and flour the pan(s) and scoop in the batter. Bake for 55–70 minutes until golden brown and a toothpick comes out clean. Cool before removing from pan(s) and frosting.

Classic Carrot Cake
(Makes 1 - 9"x13" sheet cake or 1 - 8" 2-layer cake)

Wet ingredients:
2 cups finely grated carrot (about 6 medium)
1¼ cups maple syrup
1–1¼ cups thick nut milk
⅓ cup natural light oil
2 Tbsp. liquid lecithin *or* 4 Tbsp. flax gel
2 tsp. real vanilla

Dry ingredients:
1½ cups whole wheat flour or kamut flour *or* 1⅔ cups spelt flour
1 cup kamut flour, whole wheat pastry flour *or* unbleached white flour
⅓–½ cup natural raw sugar, brown date sugar *or* natural granular sugar
3 Tbsp. powdered egg replacer
2 Tbsp. arrowroot powder *or* 2 tsp. guar gum or xanthan gum
3½–4½ tsp. no-alum baking powder
1 tsp. cinnamon
¾ tsp. sea salt
½ tsp. nutmeg
Optional: 1–2 Tbsp. gluten flour (greatly improves rising)
Optional: ½–1 cup chopped raw nuts (fresh walnuts or pecans are best)

Preheat the oven to 350°F. Mix the wet ingredients together. Sift the dry ingredients into a separate bowl. Slowly stir the dry into the wet ingredients and beat 150–200 strokes or beat with an electric mixer for 2–3 minutes. Stir in the nuts last. The mixture should be very thick and barely pourable. Add extra flour or nut milk if necessary. Lightly oil and flour the pan(s) and scoop in the thick mixture. Bake for 50–65 minutes until golden brown and a toothpick comes out clean. Cool the cake before removing from the pan(s) and frosting. The **Coconut Frosting**, **Vanilla Nut Frosting** and **Tapioca Maple Frosting** are especially good for this cake. Keeps 5–7 days or may be frozen like other cakes.

Cinnamon Spice Cake
(Makes 1 - 9"x13" sheet cake or 1 - 8" 2-layer cake)

Wet ingredients:
1 cup maple syrup *or* fruit concentrate
1–1½ cups thick nut milk
⅔ cup natural light oil
2 Tbsp. liquid lecithin *or* 4 Tbsp. flax gel
2 tsp. real vanilla

Dry ingredients:
2 cups kamut flour or whole wheat pastry flour *or* 2¼ cups spelt flour*
1 cup unbleached white flour or whole wheat pastry flour *or* ½ cup tapioca flour and ½ cup amaranth flour
½ cup natural raw sugar, brown date sugar *or* other natural granular sugar

3 Tbsp. powdered egg replacer
2 Tbsp. arrowroot powder *or* 2 tsp. guar gum or xanthan gum
3½–4½ tsp. no-alum baking powder
1½–2 tsp. cinnamon
1 tsp. nutmeg
½–¾ tsp. sea salt
½ tsp. ground cloves
⅛–¼ tsp. ginger
Optional: 1–2 Tbsp. gluten flour (greatly improves rising)
Optional: ½ cup chopped raw nuts (fresh walnuts or pecans are best)

Follow the directions for **Classic Carrot Cake** (above).
*2 cups millet flour may be used instead of wheat if the dry or liquid sweetener is increased by ⅓–½ cup and the nutmeg and cloves are increased by ¼ tsp. each. Use 2 tsp. of cinnamon.

Happiness "Essene" Cake
(Makes 1 - 9"x9" cake)

2 cups sprouted wheat
  berries, ground
1 cup maple syrup *or* fruit
  concentrate
1 tsp. real vanilla

⅔ cup whole wheat flour
⅓ cup whole wheat pastry
  flour *or* unbleached white
  flour

1 Tbsp. no-alum baking
  powder
1 tsp. cinnamon
½ tsp. sea salt
¼ tsp. *each* ginger and
  nutmeg
Few dashes allspice

Preheat the oven to 325°F. Grind the wheat berries with a blender, grinder or food processor. Mix them with the sweetener and vanilla. Sift the remaining ingredients together in a separate bowl. Gradually stir the dry ingredients into the wet and mix well. Lightly oil and flour a 9"x9" square cake pan. Gently press the mixture into the pan. Bake for 35–50 minutes or until lightly browned. The cake may be topped with **Coconut Frosting** or another vanilla frosting if desired.

Tofu Passion Cheesecake
(Makes 1 - 9" or 10" round cake)

1½ lbs (750 g) soft tofu (if soft is unavailable, you may use regular, but it may be a bit gritty)

1 cup maple syrup *or* fruit concentrate

¼ cup natural raw sugar *or* other natural granular sugar

3 Tbsp. natural light oil

4 Tbsp. arrowroot powder

3 Tbsp. grated lemon rind *or* orange rind

2 tsp. guar gum *or* xanthan gum (*or* gluten flour, if gums are unavailable)

1 tsp. real vanilla extract

¼–½ tsp. sea salt

Optional: 8–14 drops natural lemon or orange flavouring

Optional: 1 pie crust shell

Mix all ingredients together, *except* the pie crust, in a food processor or homogenizing juicer. Line a 10" pie plate with the crust or, if no crust is used, oil a 9" pie plate. Preheat the oven to 350°F. Spread the tofu mixture evenly in the crust or the oiled pie plate, and smooth out the top so the "cheesecake" will be even. Bake for about 45 minutes or until the cake is "set" and turns a medium golden colour. Chill thoroughly and serve with **Strawberry Special Topping** or **Fruit Delight Topping**. If desired, the topping can be spread over the cool cake and chilled to add a fruit layer to the cheesecake, or the topping can just be spooned on before serving each piece.

Carob Mint Cheesecake

Follow the directions for **Tofu Passion Cheesecake** (above), but add ½ cup roasted carob powder and 8–14 drops peppermint extract along with ¼ cup extra liquid sweetener. Omit the lemon rind and flavouring.

Strawberry Special Topping

½ lb (1½–2 cups) fresh or
  frozen strawberries
¾–1 cup water

2–3 Tbsp. arrowroot powder
2–6 Tbsp. liquid sweetener

Heat the berries in half the water and mash them as they heat (or slice before heating). Mix the remaining water thoroughly with the arrowroot powder, making sure there are no lumps. Add the arrowroot mixture and sweetener to the fruit and stir constantly over medium heat until the sauce thickens and becomes bright coloured. Chill and serve with **Tofu Passion Cheesecake** or as a topping on ice cream or cakes.

Tofu Whipped Cream

8 oz (225 g) very fresh soft
  or regular plain tofu (do
  not use pressed, flavoured
  or Japanese varieties, or
  previously frozen tofu)
4–6 Tbsp. maple syrup *or*
  fruit concentrate

1–2 tsp. real vanilla
  flavouring
Optional: 2–3 tsp. arrowroot
  powder or tapioca flour *or*
  ½ tsp. guar gum or
  xanthan gum, to thicken
Optional: 1–2 dashes
  cinnamon

Rinse the tofu in cold water and press between several layers of paper or clean cloth towels to squeeze out all water possible. Break the tofu into small pieces or mash it, and put it in the blender or food processor. Add the remaining ingredients and blend. Taste and adjust flavouring if desired, then blend again if necessary. Add an optional thickener if desired. Chill and serve.

Fruit Delight Topping

Follow the directions for **Strawberry Special Topping** (page 183), but use raspberries, blueberries, sliced peaches, apricots or other similar fruits in place of the strawberries.

Tapioca Maple Frosting
(Makes 2 cups)

2 cups tapioca flour
1–1¼ cups maple syrup
3–4 tsp. real vanilla

4 Tbsp. arrowroot powder
Few dashes sea salt

Combine all the ingredients in a food processor. Chill only slightly before spreading on a cool cake. This is thick, rich frosting a bit like a glaze. Even those who don't like tapioca will love this frosting! Keeps refrigerated up to 8 days.

Vanilla Nut Frosting
(Makes 2 cups)

1 cup ground raw cashews, blanched almonds *or* pine nuts
10 oz (300 g) soft tofu
½–⅔ cup maple syrup
4 Tbsp. arrowroot powder
2 tsp. real vanilla

1½ tsp. guar gum *or* xanthan gum*
¼–½ tsp. almond extract *or* other extract, or more to taste
Few dashes sea salt

Combine all the ingredients in a food processor and mix thoroughly. Chill and spread on a cool cake. Keeps refrigerated for 5–7 days.

*If a gum is unavailable, use 3–4 Tbsp. flax gel or heat the arrowroot in 2–3 Tbsp. water or fruit juice until thickened and add to the recipe.

Coconut Frosting

1½–2 lbs (700–900 g) soft
    tofu
1–1½ cups shredded
    unsweetened coconut

1 cup or more maple syrup
    or other liquid sweetener
2–4 Tbsp. arrowroot powder
3–4 tsp. guar gum *or*
    xanthan gum*

In a food processor, mix all ingredients until smooth. Chill thoroughly and spread on a cool cake. Keeps 4–7 days refrigerated.

    *If a gum is unavailable, heat 4–6 Tbsp. arrowroot (instead of the 2–4 Tbsp.) with ¼ cup coconut milk or water, on medium heat, until thickened. Then add the remaining ingredients and chill.

Banana Nut Frosting

Follow the directions for **Vanilla Nut Frosting** (above), but omit the maple syrup and add 1–1½ cups mashed banana. ½ tsp. cinnamon may also be added if desired. Add 2–3 tsp. lemon juice.

Carob Nut Frosting

Follow the directions for **Vanilla Nut Frosting** (above), but add ⅓–½ cup carob powder and use the extra maple syrup and/or extra water or juice to obtain the desired consistency. Add ¼–½ tsp. or more peppermint extract if desired for added flavour.

Carob Fudge Topping

⅔ cup thick **Nut Milk**
⅓ cup maple syrup *or* fruit
    concentrate
¼ cup carob powder (dark
    roasted or regular)

2 tsp. arrowroot powder
Dash or two of sea salt
½ tsp. real vanilla flavouring

Blend all ingredients *except* the vanilla. Bring to a boil and simmer 5 minutes on medium-low heat, stirring constantly, until the mixture thickens. Add vanilla. Remove from heat and serve hot or chilled as a topping for cakes, brownies, ice creams and other desserts.

Note: If vanilla extract is used instead of flavouring, it should be heated with the rest of the ingredients.

Carob Syrup

Follow the directions for **Carob Fudge Topping** (above), but omit the arrowroot powder. The mixture will thicken only slightly when heated. Use 3–4 Tbsp. of cold syrup to flavour 1 cup of chilled milk substitute. Mix well before drinking. Delicious, especially in cold, plain, **Thick Nut Milk**. Some people like this better than chocolate milk!

Cookies, Candies, Puddings, Pies, Ice Creams

Pecan Spice Cookies
(Makes 1–1½ dozen)

¼ cup natural light oil
½ cup maple syrup *or* other liquid sweetener
¼ cup barley malt powder, brown date sugar *or* other natural powdered or granular sweetener

¾ cup flour: kamut, whole wheat, spelt *or* millet
½ cup light flour: unbleached white *or* tapioca

¾–1 cup chopped raw pecans
½ cup raisins, currants *or* chopped dates
1 tsp. anise seeds
½–1 tsp. cinnamon
⅛ tsp. sea salt

Optional: several dashes *each* nutmeg, ginger and cloves
Optional: ¼–½ cup shredded unsweetened coconut

Preheat the oven to 400°F. Mix the oil and sweeteners together well. In a separate bowl, mix the remaining ingredients, then slowly stir them into the liquid mixture. For each cookie, drop 1–2 Tbsp. of the dough on lightly oiled cookie sheets, about 2"–3" apart. Bake for 9–12 minutes, until lightly browned but still soft. Cool on wire racks. The cookies get crispy as they cool.

Almond Crunch Cookies
(Makes about 1½ dozen)

Wet ingredients:
½ cup maple syrup *or* fruit concentrate
3 Tbsp. natural light or almond oil
1 Tbsp. almond butter
1–2 tsp. real vanilla flavouring
Dry ingredients:
1¼ cup kamut flour *or* ¾ cup whole wheat flour and ½ cup whole wheat pastry flour or unbleached white flour

¼ cup natural raw sugar, brown date sugar *or* other granular natural sugar
¼ cup sliced or chopped almonds
2 Tbsp. ground almonds
1 tsp. *each* no-alum baking powder and cinnamon
½–1 tsp. almond extract
⅛ tsp. sea salt

Preheat the oven to 375°F. Combine the wet ingredients thoroughly. In a separate bowl, sift together the dry ingredients. Add the dry ingredients to the wet and mix well. Flatten a handful of batter to ½" and smooth into a basic round shape on a well-oiled cookie sheet, or roll out with a rolling pin and cut with cookie cutters. Whole almonds or natural candies can be used to decorate each one if desired. Bake 12–15 minutes and let the cookies cool on wire racks. The cookies will be soft and lightly browned when taken from the oven. They harden as they cool. Whole almonds or natural candies can be used to decorate each one if desired.

Carrot-Raisin Cookies

Follow the directions for **Almond Crunch Cookies** (above) but omit all the almonds and almond butter and extract. Add ½–⅔ cup finely grated carrot and ¼–⅓ cup raisins or currants to the recipe.

Double Carob Chip Cookies

Follow the directions for **Almond Crunch Cookies** (above) but omit the almonds, almond butter and extract. Substitute ¼–½ cup carob powder for the same amount of flour. Add ⅓–½ cup carob chips and 2–3 Tbsp. extra liquid sweetener. For a more "chocolatey" flavour, add 2 tsp. instant coffee substitute.

Delectable Carob Fudge

1¼ cups maple syrup *or* fruit concentrate

1 cup peanut butter, sesame tahini *or* nut butter

1–1¼ cups sifted carob powder

½–1 cup sesame seeds, shredded coconut *or* chopped nuts

8–14 drops peppermint extract, or to taste

2 Tbsp. arrowroot powder

1–2 tsp. real vanilla

Heat the liquid sweetener and nut butter on low to medium heat until hot and soft. Remove from heat and stir in the remaining ingredients. Press the mixture into a 9" or 10" glass pie plate or similar pan and press extra coconut or nuts on top. Chill thoroughly. Cut and serve. Keeps up to 3 months refrigerated.

Date Candy Surprise

Dates—pitted (sticky variety)

Almonds or hazelnuts

Pecans or walnuts

Cashews

Coconut—shredded unsweetened

Flatten one medium or large date, or press two small dates together, so the sticky side is on top. Press 2 or 3 different nuts into the top, then press the whole flat date candy into the coconut. Press coconut firmly into the top and bottom of each candy. Chill before use. Keeps for many weeks.

Apple Crisp Delight
(Serves 4)

6–8 medium baking apples, cored and peeled or unpeeled
⅓ cup apple juice *or* orange juice
⅓–½ cup maple syrup, fruit concentrate *or* other liquid sweetener

¼–⅓ cup rolled oats
½–1 tsp. cinnamon
Several dashes *each* ginger, nutmeg and sea salt
Optional: ¼–½ cup chopped nuts
Optional: ¼–½ cup raisins *or* currants

Preheat the oven to 350°F. Cut the apples into quarters, then cut each quarter into 4–5 chunks. Place the pieces evenly in a lightly oiled, shallow 9" or 10" glass or enamel baking dish. (Do *not* use metal pan!) Pour the juice and liquid sweetener evenly over the apples. Then sprinkle on the oats and spices. Bake for 30–40 minutes or until the apples are as tender as you like them. Only add the nuts and/or dried fruit during the last 10 minutes of baking time for the best flavour and to insure they are not overcooked and burnt. Enjoy this easy dessert or snack often.

Rolled Pie Crust
(Makes 1 double or 2 single pie crusts)

Dry ingredients:
2 cups kamut flour *or* 1¼ cups whole wheat flour and ¾ cup unbleached white flour or whole wheat pastry flour
1 Tbsp. arrowroot powder *or* 1–2 tsp. guar gum or xanthan gum

¾–1 tsp. sea salt

Wet ingredients:
⅔ cup natural light oil
¼ cup cold water
1–2 tsp. liquid lecithin
Optional: 1–2 tsp. liquid sweetener

Mix the wet and dry ingredients separately. Add the dry ingredients to the wet and mix with a fork or pastry blender. Knead the dough for a couple of minutes and divide into two parts. Roll one part between 2 pieces of wax paper, until it is about ⅛" thick and 11–12" in diameter. While rolling out the dough, be careful to turn it upside down once in a while, and lift the wax paper from the rolled dough on each side occasionally, so it will not stick permanently to the dough. Dust it with a bit of extra flour as needed to further insure that it will not stick. Lightly oil a 9" or 10" pie pan. Remove one layer of wax paper from the rolled dough and turn it upside down over the pie pan. Gently remove the top, last layer of wax paper and shape the pie crust to the pan; do not stretch the dough or it will shrink and grow smaller while the pie is baking. Use a fork to poke air holes in the dough.

Preheat the oven to 425°F. After shaping the bottom crust, fill it with pie filling and cover it with the second rolled-out pie crust. Flute the edges together, make a few slits or fork holes in the top crust, and then bake for 30–40 minutes, or according to filling directions, until golden and flaky. Serve pie hot or chilled.

Granola Crust

Use about half a batch of unbaked **Granola** without large nut or seed chunks or dried fruit. Press it into an oiled pie pan and bake at 350°F for 10–14 minutes until toasty but not quite browned. Cool and fill with pie filling that does not require baking. Or leave unbaked for **Home Apple Pie** or other pie that requires baking.

Graham Cracker or Cookie Crust
(Makes 1 - 9" or 10" pie crust)

1¾ cups graham cracker crumbs *or* plain cookie crumbs, finely crumbled

¼ cup natural light oil

¼ cup maple syrup *or* other light liquid sweetener

1 Tbsp. arrowroot powder *or* 1–2 tsp. guar gum or xanthan gum

1 tsp. cinnamon

Optional: several dashes sea salt

Mix everything together thoroughly with a fork. Lightly oil a 9" or 10" pie pan and press the mixture evenly into the bottom and sides of the pan, saving a bit of the mixture to sprinkle on top of the pie if desired. Press the crust firmly and evenly to insure a solid crust. The crust will be about ¼" thick or thinner. Chill it 1 hour before adding filling. Use for cold, no-bake pies, or bake according to the pie filling directions. Crust will keep well refrigerated 1–3 days before filling and up to 7 or 8 days after filling.

Home Apple Pie

6–8 large baking apples, peeled, cored and chopped

Optional: ½ cup raisins, currants, raw pecans *or* fresh walnuts

¼ cup water

2½ Tbsp. arrowroot powder

¼ tsp. sea salt

½–¾ cup maple syrup

1–2 Tbsp. lemon juice

1½–2 tsp. cinnamon

1 double **Rolled Pie Crust**

Simmer the apples and optionals with the water on medium heat for 8–10 minutes or until tender. Drain the apples and save the liquid. Quick-cool the liquid and mix it with the arrowroot powder and sea salt. Heat it in a saucepan until it thickens, stirring constantly. Preheat the oven to 425°F. Mix the apples, arrowroot mixture and remaining ingredients together and scoop into a bottom pie crust. Add a top crust, following the directionsfor **Rolled Pie Crust**, and bake for 30–40 minutes until browned and set. Cool pie slightly before slicing. Keeps 6–8 days refrigerated.

Lemon Creme Pie

Filling:
3 cups pineapple juice
½ cup raw ground cashews
  or ground blanched
  almonds
½ cup tapioca flour
¼ cup natural granular
  sweetener
1 Tbsp. arrowroot powder
2 Tbsp. maple syrup
2 Tbsp. grated lemon rind

Few dashes sea salt
Optional: Several drops
  natural lemon flavouring
3 Tbsp. fresh lemon juice

1 single **Rolled Pie Crust**,
  baked, *or* 1 **Graham
  Cracker Crust**
Optional: **Tofu Whipped
  Cream *or* Coconut
  Frosting** for topping

Blend all filling ingredients *except* the lemon juice until smooth. Heat the mixture on medium-high heat, stirring constantly, until thickened like a paste. Then add the lemon juice and mix well. Place in a crust and chill until firm. Slice and serve with topping if desired. Keeps up to 6–7 days refrigerated.

Easy Pineapple Pie

3 cups pineapple chunks, drained

1/3 cup maple syrup *or* fruit concentrate

6 Tbsp. arrowroot powder

3 Tbsp. natural granular sweetener

2 tsp. guar gum or xanthan gum*

Few dashes each sea salt and ginger

1 single **Rolled Pie Crust**

Optional: **Tofu Whipped Cream** or **Coconut Frosting** for topping

Blend the first six ingredients together and place in the pie crust. Chill until firm and serve with one of the toppings, **Creamy Vanilla Tofu Ice Cream** or **Granola**.

*If a gum is unavailable, stir the filling ingredients together on medium-low heat until the mixture starts to thicken, then chill.

Berry Berry Pie

4 Tbsp. arrowroot powder

1/4 cup apple, peach, pear *or* white grape juice

1–1 1/4 lbs fresh or frozen strawberries, raspberries, blackberries *or* blueberries

1/3–1/2 cup maple syrup

2 Tbsp. natural granular or raw sweetener

1–1 1/2 tsp. guar gum *or* xanthan gum*

Few dashes sea salt

Optional: 1–3 tsp. fresh lemon juice

1 single pie crust

Mix the arrowroot into the fruit juice completely, then mix it with the remaining ingredients. Cook over medium-high heat, stirring constantly, until thickened. Let the mixture cool a few minutes, then scoop it into the pie crust and chill. Serve with ice cream or Tofu Whipped Cream. Keeps 7–8 days refrigerated.

*If a gum is unavailable, it may be omitted.

Rice and Raisin Pudding

2 cups cooked brown rice, cold

⅔ cup thick nut milk *or* sweet fruit juice (apple, pear, peach or apricot are good)

½–⅔ cup maple syrup *or* fruit concentrate

2 Tbsp. arrowroot powder

2–3 tsp. grated lemon rind *or* orange rind

2 tsp. real vanilla

1–1½ tsp. cinnamon

1 tsp. guar gum *or* xanthan gum

⅛ tsp. sea salt

Optional: ½–⅔ cup raisins, currants, chopped dates *or* chopped nuts

1 cup of dry brown rice makes about 2 cups cooked brown rice. But be sure to measure after cooking, as rice varieties expand differently. Use sweet brown rice if available.

Preheat the oven to 375°F. Combine all ingredients carefully with a fork so as not to mash the rice. Mix thoroughly. Spread the mixture in a lightly oiled 9"x9" casserole dish and bake 35–45 minutes, uncovered, until "set" and somewhat firm. Serve this tasty, nutritious dessert hot or cold.

*Sweetener may be reduced for special diets or for a breakfast cereal version of this recipe.

Sensational Carob Mint Tofu Pudding
(Makes about 4 servings)

1 lb (450 g) soft tofu (or regular if soft is unavailable)
1–1½ cups maple syrup *or* fruit concentrate
½–⅔ cup carob powder*
2–3 Tbsp. arrowroot powder

3 tsp. real vanilla flavouring
8–14 drops peppermint extract, or more to taste
Several dashes sea salt
Optional: shredded unsweetened coconut

Combine all ingredients in a food processor or homogenizing juicer. (This mixture is too thick for a blender.) Coconut may be added before or after processing. Spoon into individual pudding cups and chill thoroughly until set: about 15 minutes in the freezer or 1 hour in the refrigerator. A rich dessert. Most people think the carob in this pudding tastes exactly like chocolate!

Creamy Carob Fondue

1 cup maple syrup, fruit concentrate *or* other liquid sweetener
1 cup peanut butter, sesame tahini *or* nut butter
⅓–½ cup carob powder (dark roasted or regular)
1 tsp. real vanilla
Couple dashes sea salt

Optional: 8–14 drops peppermint extract
Rice cakes, spelt cakes or other puffed whole grain wafers, broken into small pieces for dipping
Cut fruit pieces: apples, pears, bananas, peaches, apricots, strawberries, etc.
Whole raw nuts

Mix all the ingredients *except* for the rice cakes, nuts and fruit, and heat in a saucepot or fondue pot until hot as you like it. Dip the puffed cakes and/or fruit pieces in the sauce for a tasty and nutritious snack or dessert. Keeps refrigerated many weeks.

Thanks to Dr. Pia Longstaffe, D.C., for the original recipe.

Agar Agar Fruit Jello

¼ oz (about 6–7 Tbsp.) agar agar flakes *or* 2–2½ Tbsp. agar agar powder
1 cup cool water

1–1½ qts (L) fruit juice (apple, pear, peach, apricot, papaya, grape, strawberry, sweet cherry, etc.*), at room temperature
Optional: cut fruits

Mix the agar flakes in the water and heat to boiling on medium-high heat, stirring as it heats. Once it boils, turn down the heat and simmer until most of the agar is dissolved and it thickens. Stir regularly. Make sure the fruit juice is at room temperature or just a little bit warmer. Pour the juice into a 2-qt (2-L) glass or metal bowl and *strain* the agar mixture into it with a fine-mesh metal or plastic strainer. Stir it and mix everything well. Chill thoroughly until it gels. When it is partially set, about 30–40 minutes or more, add cut fruits to it if desired. Jello is usually ready to eat in 1½–3 hours. Some juice may settle to the bottom of the bowl when the jello is spooned out—this is natural for agar jello.

*Most citrus juices do not "set well" with agar. Avoid them, or use just a little mixed with other juices.

Agar is a great gelatin substitute. This jello also makes a nice topping for ice cream.

Frozen Fruit Slushes and Ices

Choose one or two fruits and freeze them solid. Try berries, bananas, mangos, papayas, kiwis, pears, peaches, apricots, pineapple, citrus fruits, cherries, avocados or other fruits suitable for freezing. Add just enough liquid sweetener or fruit juice to the frozen fruit so that it will blend or process easily and taste sweet enough for a dessert. Add a few dashes of sea salt and vanilla, rum, maple or other flavouring if desired. Freeze the mixture solid. Break the frozen mixture into chunks and soften with a food processor or homogenizing juicer. Re-freeze until it is totally solid, then process the mixture again and enjoy as a fruit "slush" or keep frozen for later and enjoy as an ice. Remove the ice from the freezer a few minutes before serving to soften.

Rich Vanilla Ice Cream

2 cups water
¾ cup ground raw cashew
    pieces *or* ground blanched
    almonds
⅓ cup maple syrup

3 Tbsp. arrowroot powder
3 tsp. real vanilla extract*
1 tsp. slippery elm powder *or*
    guar gum
3 dashes sea salt

Blend all the ingredients thoroughly in a blender until smooth. Freeze the mixture solid. Cut into pieces and use a food processor or homogenizing juicer to chop it, soften it and mix it thoroughly for a smoother, more uniform texture. Re-freeze the ice cream, remove it from the freezer several minutes before serving to soften slightly, and enjoy. This vanilla ice cream has exquisite flavour.

    *You may substitute vanilla flavouring for real vanilla extract, but the flavour will not be quite as good. If desired, ground nuts may be increased to 1 cup and maple syrup to ½ cup for even richer ice cream.

Carob Ice Cream

2 cups water
½ cup carob powder (dark
    roasted is best)
½ cup ground raw cashew
    pieces *or* blanched
    almonds
⅓–½ cup maple syrup *or*
    fruit concentrate
3 Tbsp. arrowroot powder

1 tsp. real vanilla extract
1 tsp. slippery elm powder *or*
    guar gum
3–4 dashes sea salt
Optional: 10–16 drops
    peppermint flavouring
Optional: 1 tsp. instant
    coffee substitute

Follow the directions for **Rich Vanilla Ice Cream** (above).

Creamy Vanilla Tofu Ice Cream
(Makes 2½–3 cups)

10 oz (300 g) soft tofu
½–¾ cup maple syrup
2 Tbsp. arrowroot powder
4–6 tsp. real vanilla
1 tsp. guar gum *or* slippery
   elm powder

Few dashes sea salt
Optional, for added
   richness: ¼ cup ground
   raw cashews or blanched
   almonds

Combine all the ingredients in a food processor or blender and freeze solid. Defrost for 5–10 minutes and use a food processor or homogenizing juicer to soften the mixture. Mix it again. Freeze a second time. Remove from the freezer a few minutes before serving. Add fruit or carob topping, granola or nuts if desired.

Carob Mint Tofu Ice Cream

Follow the directions for **Creamy Vanilla Tofu Ice Cream** (above), but use the extra maple syrup or added fruit juice and add ⅓–½ cup carob powder along with ¼–½ tsp. or more peppermint extract. Do not add the extra ground nuts.

Carob Chip Ice Cream

Follow the directions for either of the carob ice creams (above), but add ½–¾ cup carob chips.

Banana Tofu Ice Cream

Follow the directions for **Creamy Vanilla Tofu Ice Cream** (above). Use only ¼ cup maple syrup and add 1–1½ cups mashed banana along with ½ tsp. cinnamon if desired. Instead of ground nuts, add ¼–½ cup chopped **Home Roasted Nuts** of your choice or omit the nuts altogether.

Kiwi Tofu Ice Cream Sensation
(Makes 4 cups)

6–7 large kiwis, peeled and chopped

20 oz (600 g) soft tofu

⅓–½ cup maple syrup, fruit concentrate *or* other liquid sweetener

2 tsp. real vanilla extract or flavouring

1 tsp. slippery elm powder *or* guar gum

Optional: couple dashes sea salt

Optional: 1–2 Tbsp. fresh beet juice, for a redder colour

Mix everything together in a food processor, or mix and put it through a homogenizing juicer. Freeze solid. Process again or put through the juicer again. Freeze a second time and enjoy. Remove from freezer several minutes before serving to soften slightly. Keeps frozen many weeks. Delicious and high in calcium, potassium and protein too!

Avocado Tofu Ice Cream

Follow the directions for **Kiwi Tofu Ice Cream Sensation** (above), but substitute 2½–3 cups avocado (about 4 medium) for the kiwis. Also increase the liquid sweetener to ½–¾ cup. *Optional*: Add 2–3 tsp. fresh lemon juice to the avocado to help it retain its bright colour and stay fresh.

Raspberry or Strawberry Tofu Ice Cream
(Makes 4 cups)

2½–3 cups sliced raspberries *or* strawberries, fresh or frozen

20 oz (600 g) soft tofu

⅓–½ cup maple syrup, fruit concentrate *or* other liquid sweetener

2 tsp. real vanilla extract or flavouring

1 tsp. slippery elm powder *or* guar gum

Optional: couple dashes sea salt

Optional: 1–2 Tbsp. fresh beet juice for a redder colour

Mix everything together in a food processor, or mix and put it through a homogenizing juicer. Freeze solid. Process again or put through the juicer again. Freeze a second time and enjoy. Remove from freezer several minutes before serving to soften slightly. Keeps frozen many weeks. Delicious and high in calcium, potassium and protein too!

Peach or Apricot Tofu Ice Cream

Follow the directions for **Raspberry or Strawberry Tofu Ice Cream** (above), but use 2½–3 cups sliced fresh peaches or apricots instead of the berries. Omit the beet juice. Instead, 2–3 tsp. grated orange rind and/or 8–12 drops real orange flavouring may be added for a special flavour.

Classic Ice Cream Variations

Use fresh fruits, shredded coconut, nuts, raisins, organic citrus rind, other flavourings, etc. in the ice cream. Experiment and create your own.

Breads

Country Cornbread

Dry ingredients:
1 cup cornmeal
½ cup whole wheat, kamut
  or spelt flour*
½ cup unbleached white *or*
  whole wheat pastry flour*
2–3 Tbsp. powdered egg
  replacer
2 Tbsp. arrowroot powder
3–4 tsp. no-alum baking
  powder

2 tsp. gluten flour *or* 1 tsp.
  guar gum or xanthan gum
¾–1 tsp. sea salt

Wet ingredients:
¾ cup thick **Nut Milk, Soy
  Milk** *or* other milk
  substitute
⅓ cup natural light oil
3 Tbsp. liquid sweetener
1–2 Tbsp. liquid lecithin *or*
  3–4 Tbsp. flax gel

Preheat the oven to 400°F. Mix the dry and wet ingredients separately. Slowly add the dry mixture to the wet, mixing carefully. Scoop into a lightly oiled and floured 8"x8" pan and bake for about 30–35 minutes or more before slicing. Makes 16 - 2" pieces. Keeps 2–3 days at a cool room temperature or 5–7 days refrigerated, but cornbread tastes best the first and second days. Reheat in foil wrap for the best flavour after day 2.

   *The 1 cup whole wheat flour may be omitted if 2 cups of very finely ground cornmeal are used in the recipe instead of 1. The second 1 cup wheat flour may be replaced by oat flour.

Flatbreads
(Makes 8)

½ cup flour: whole wheat, kamut, spelt, buckwheat, millet or amaranth

½ cup light flour: unbleached white, brown rice or tapioca

2 tsp. arrowroot powder

2 tsp. natural light oil

½ cup water

⅓–⅔ cup extra flour, for kneading

Stir the flours with the arrowroot powder. In a separate bowl, mix the oil and water, then add to the flour mixture. Work the dough with a fork and then your hands. Knead briefly and roll into a ball. Divide the ball into 8 parts. Roll each part into a ball and pat flat. Sprinkle each bread with flour and roll between 2 sheets of wax paper with a rolling pin. Turn frequently while rolling, and lift the wax paper occasionally to add flour so the dough does not stick. The bread should be somewhat rounded and about ⅛" thick. (Wax paper may not be needed if whole wheat and/or unbleached white flours are used.)

Preheat the oven to 400°F. Lightly oil a frying pan and heat to medium-high. Put one flatbread in the pan and heat 15–20 seconds on each side. Immediately put bread in the oven, on the wire racks, and heat 3 minutes. Turn over and heat 1½–2 minutes longer. The bread will puff up a bit in the oven, but not as much as a traditional pita because it has no yeast. Re-oil the pan with a paper towel dipped in oil, and repeat the procedure for each flatbread. Cool breads before storing or eat them hot from the oven.

Soda Bread
(Makes 1 loaf)

Dry ingredients:
2 cups whole wheat flour
2 cups whole wheat pastry
  flour *or* 1 cup whole
  wheat, rye or other flour
  and 1 cup unbleached
  white flour
2 Tbsp. powdered egg
  replacer
2 Tbsp. arrowroot powder
2 tsp. baking soda
1½–2 tsp. no-alum baking
  powder
1 tsp. sea salt
Optional: 2–3 tsp. gluten
  flour

Wet ingredients:
1½ cups water
3–4 Tbsp. maple syrup, fruit
  concentrate *or* other
  liquid sweetener
3–4 Tbsp. natural light oil
2 Tbsp. apple cider vinegar
1 Tbsp. liquid lecithin *or* 4
  Tbsp. flax gel (reduce the
  water by 2 Tbsp. if flax gel
  is used)
¼ cup ground raw cashew
  pieces or ground
  blanched almonds

Preheat the oven to 375°F. Sift the dry ingredients together. Blend the wet ingredients with the ground nuts. Slowly add the dry ingredients to the wet and mix with a spoon or fork. As the batter stiffens, mix with the hands. Knead 1–2 minutes on a flat surface. Shape the loaf into a round shape for a 8"x8" shallow baking pan or into a long loaf for a large bread pan. Rub a little extra oil over the loaf while shaping. Lightly oil and flour the pan. Bake for 55–60 minutes. Cool 5 minutes. Remove from the pan and cool another 30 minutes or so before slicing. Keeps 4–7 days refrigerated.

Quick Garlic Bread

½ cup natural light oil
6–10 cloves garlic, minced

1 tsp. raw white onion,
 minced
⅛ tsp. sea salt, or to taste

Blend all ingredients and brush or spoon generously on **Flatbreads, Soda Bread** or your favourite bread. Wrap the bread in foil and warm it in a 400°F oven for 15–25 minutes until hot.

Beautiful Banana Bread
(Makes 1 large loaf)

Dry ingredients:
2 cups kamut flour *or* 1¼
 cups whole wheat flour
 and ¾ cup whole wheat
 pastry or unbleached
 white flour
3–4 tsp. no-alum baking
 powder
¼ tsp. sea salt

Wet ingredients:
2 cups mashed banana
½ cup maple syrup *or* other
 liquid sweetener
⅓–½ cup milk substitute *or*
 fruit juice (apple, peach,
 pear)
¼ cup natural light oil
1–2 tsp. real vanilla

Optional: ½ cup chopped
 nuts *or* dried fruit

Preheat the oven to 350°F. Mix the wet and dry ingredients separately. Sift the dry ingredients slowly into the wet. Add extra liquid only if needed to make a stiff but stirrable batter. Scoop the mixture into a large, lightly oiled and floured loaf pan and bake for 55–65 minutes until nicely browned on top and a toothpick comes out clean. Wait at least 15 minutes before removing from the pan. Cool completely before slicing. Keeps 6–8 days in a cool place or refrigerated. May be frozen.

Variations:

Johnny Apple Bread: Follow the directions for **Beautiful Banana Bread** but substitute applesauce and apple juice for the bananas and liquid. Add 1 tsp. cinnamon.

Date Nut Bread: Follow the directions for **Beautiful Banana Bread** but add 1 cup chopped dates and 1 cup chopped pecans or other raw nuts.

Create your own breads!

Banana Nut Rice Bread
(Makes 1 loaf)

Dry ingredients:
1¼ cups brown rice flour
1 cup rice bran (stabilized bran is best)
2 Tbsp. arrowroot powder *or* egg replacer
3 tsp. no-alum baking powder
1 tsp. cinnamon *or* allspice
¾ tsp. sea salt

Wet ingredients:
1½ cups mashed ripe banana (about 3 medium)
½ cup maple syrup *or* fruit concentrate
¼ cup natural light oil
2 Tbsp. liquid lecithin, *and/or* 2 tsp. guar gum added to dry ingredients
2 tsp. real vanilla

Preheat the oven to 325°F and lightly oil a loaf pan. (Avoid non-stick pans as they bake gluten-free breads unevenly.) Sift the dry ingredients together, then add them to the wet just before baking. Mix well to make a thick but stirrable batter. Scoop the batter into the loaf pan. Smooth the top of the loaf. Bake 85–90 minutes and cool 45–60 minutes before removing from the pan. Slice carefully as this is a delicate, delicious gluten-free bread.

Pumpkin Pecan Bread

2 cups kamut flour *or* 1¼
  cups whole wheat flour
  and ¾ cup whole wheat
  pastry or unbleached
  white flour
3–4 tsp. no-alum baking
  powder
1 tsp. cinnamon
¼ tsp. *each* sea salt, nutmeg
  and ginger

½–1 cup broken raw pecans
1 cup cooked and mashed
  pumpkin
¾–1 cup maple syrup *or*
  fruit concentrate
¼–⅓ cup apple juice
¼ cup natural light oil
2 tsp. real vanilla

Sift all dry ingredients together except for the nuts. Mix the wet ingredients separately. Lightly oil and flour a bread pan. Preheat the oven to 350°F. Mix all the ingredients together thoroughly to make a slightly stiff batter. Use extra juice only if it is too dry, add flour if it is too thin. Scoop the mixture into the pan and smooth the top. Bake 60–65 minutes until browned and a toothpick comes out clean. Cool 30 minutes before removing from the pan to a rack. Let cool completely on the rack before slicing. Keeps 5–7 days refrigerated, or may be frozen.

Zucchini-Carrot Bread or Muffins

Wet ingredients:

½ cup cooked quinoa
(2½–3 Tbsp. dry makes ½
cup cooked)*

½ cup zucchini, finely
grated and towel dried

½ cup finely grated carrot,
well packed

½ cup crushed pineapple,
drained

¾ cup maple syrup *or* fruit
juice concentrate

¼ cup natural light oil

½ cup apple, pear or peach
juice

1–2 tsp. real vanilla

Optional: ½ cup raisins *or*
chopped nuts

Dry ingredients:

2 cups kamut flour *or* 1¼
cups whole wheat flour
and ¾ cup unbleached
white flour or whole
wheat pastry flour

3–4 tsp. no-alum baking
powder

¼ tsp. sea salt

Cook the quinoa for 18–20 minutes. Preheat the oven to 350°F. Mix all the wet ingredients together in one bowl. In a separate bowl, sift the flour, baking powder and salt together. Lightly oil a bread or loaf pan, line just the bottom with wax paper and oil the top of the paper as well. Lightly flour the pan and shake out the excess flour. Add the dry ingredients to the wet and mix completely. The batter will be slightly stiff but stirrable. Scoop it into the pan immediately and shape it until it is smooth on top and even in the corners. Bake for about 55–60 minutes until lightly browned and a toothpick comes out clean. Cool for about 15 minutes before cutting and removing from the pan. For muffins, bake at 375°–400°F for 20–40 minutes until browned.

*Millet or another grain may be used instead of quinoa.

Easy Holiday Fruitcake

1 cup raisins *or* currants
1 cup dates, chopped
1 cup prunes *or* figs,
  chopped
1 cup dried apricots,
  chopped
1 cup dried pears *or*
  pineapple, chopped
1–1½ cups pecans *or* fresh
  walnuts, chopped
1 cup apple cider, at room
  temperature

½ cup natural light oil
¾–1 cup maple syrup *or*
  fruit concentrate
2 Tbsp. liquid lecithin
1 tsp. sea salt
Optional: (but adds lots of
  flavour) 1–2 tsp. rum
  flavouring or extract
1–2 tsp. grated lemon rind

¾–1 cup very warm apple
  cider *or* apple juice (about
  110°–115°F)
2 Tbsp. baking yeast

2½ cups kamut flour *or* 1½
  cups whole wheat flour
  and 1 cup unbleached
  white flour or whole
  wheat pastry flour
1 cup amaranth or
  buckwheat flour (for
  darker fruitcake) *or* 1 cup
  kamut, whole wheat,
  millet, brown rice or oat
  flour (for lighter fruitcake)
2 Tbsp. arrowroot powder *or*
  2 tsp. guar gum or
  xanthan gum
4 Tbsp. powdered egg
  replacer

Even those who don't like fruitcake will love this delicious cross between cake and fruitcake. In one bowl mix the chopped dried fruits and nuts with the apple cider. Mix well until the fruits absorb most of the liquid, and let it sit a while. In another bowl, mix the oil with the liquid sweetener, lecithin, sea salt, rum flavouring and lemon rind and mix well.

Put the warmed apple cider in a smaller bowl, add the yeast, stir well with a wire whisk and set aside for about 10 minutes. While the yeast is getting ready, add the dried fruit mixture to the sweetened oil mixture along with all the flour, arrowroot and powdered egg replacer. Mix well. A very stiff but stirrable dough will form. Then add the yeast mixture and combine everything thoroughly to make a loose batter. Place it in a bowl twice its size, cover with a damp towel and let it rise for 1½–2 hours in a warm place. After rising, stir well but carefully, so as not to rip the developed gluten. Spread batter into an oiled and floured 9"x13" pan. Let rise ½ hour, *no longer*, or it may fall in the oven.

Preheat the oven to 350°F and bake fruitcake for 45–55 minutes until nicely browned. Cool before removing from the pan. Keeps refrigerated 7–14 days, or may be frozen.

Special Recipes

Natural Ketchup

12 oz (398 mL) tomato paste
or **Tomato Sauce***
2–3 Tbsp. apple cider
vinegar
1–3 Tbsp. liquid sweetener
1 tsp. dried parsley, crushed

¼–½ tsp. tamari soy sauce
⅛ tsp. *each* basil (crushed)
and paprika
Few dashes *each* cayenne
pepper and sea kelp
Sea salt to taste

Heat everything with a little water to thin if desired. Simmer on low heat for 15 or more minutes and cool and refrigerate. Keeps 1–3 weeks refrigerated, depending on how well you keep it bacteria-free.

*Ketchup made with tomato paste is thicker and spreadable; made with **Tomato Sauce** is thinner.

Veggie Butter

½ lb (225 g) lecithin spread*
(sold in health food stores)
½ small green pepper *or* ½
stalk celery, chopped fine
5 Tbsp. tomato paste *or* 6
Tbsp. mashed, steamed
carrot with optional 1–2
tsp. mashed, steamed beet

1–2 Tbsp. white *or* yellow
onion, minced
1 Tbsp. parsley
1 tsp. *each* garlic powder,
oregano and dill weed
½ tsp. basil
Optional: sea salt *or* vegetable
sea salt, to taste

Combine all ingredients in a food processor or homogenizing juicer. Chill well before using. Keeps refrigerated for 1–2 weeks with the lecithin spread, or may be frozen. Keeps 4–7 days refrigerated if tofu is used.

*6 oz (175 g) regular tofu mixed with 2 Tbsp. natural oil can be used instead of the lecithin spread.

Tofu Mayonnaise

1 lb (450 g) regular tofu
½ cup raw cashew pieces *or* blanched almonds, ground
½ cup water
¼–⅓ cup fresh lemon juice
1 Tbsp. maple syrup *or* fruit concentrate

2–3 tsp. arrowroot powder *or* ½ tsp. guar gum or xanthan gum
1 tsp. sea salt
Optional: ½–1 tsp. white miso *and/or* onion powder

In a blender or food processor, combine all ingredients thoroughly. Chill completely and use like regular mayonnaise in recipes. Keeps 5–7 days refrigerated.

Pumpkin for Recipes

There are several ways to prepare cooked, mashed pumpkin* for recipes. Place a small whole pumpkin in a large pot half filled with water. Bring to a boil, then simmer on medium-low heat, covered, for 1–2 hours. Turn the pumpkin over when the bottom side is tender and cook until completely tender. Then seed and peel it. Drain off excess liquid and mash it by hand or in a food processor. *Or:* cut a large pumpkin into large pieces, seed it, bake it at 375°–400°F for 45–70 minutes until very tender, then peel and mash. Canned pumpkin may also be used, although it is not as fresh, nutritious or flavourful.

*Some kinds of winter squash, such as butternut or buttercup squash, may be substituted for pumpkin as they have a similar flavour.

Home Roasted Nuts

Chopped or slivered raw nuts may be roasted in a dry pan in a preheated oven at 300°F for 4–8 minutes, depending on the size of the nuts and how thinly they are layered. Stir them every minute or so and turn them as needed until lightly browned and hot.

Whole nuts like almonds and hazelnuts (filberts) can be roasted in a preheated oven at 350°F for 6–10 minutes. Use these in recipes or as a garnish or snack. Store in the refrigerator for up to several weeks.

Roasted Chestnuts

Choose fresh, firm, unwrinkled chestnuts with no signs of mold. On the flat side of each chestnut make 2 cuts with a small, sharp knife, from one end to the other in the shape of an X. Place the chestnuts, cut side up, on a low baking sheet with a thin layer of water on the bottom. Bake the chestnuts for 25–40 minutes at 350°F until browned and the cuts peel back naturally from the heat. Test one chestnut to be sure its "meat" is tender. When tender, remove from oven, cool only slightly, peel and enjoy or use in recipes. Some people like to boil the cut chestnuts for easier peeling. This is okay, though some nutrients and flavour will be lost.

Gomashio (Sesame Salt)

1–2 cups white hulled sesame seeds	3 Tbsp.–½ cup sea salt
	Optional: 1–2 tsp. sea kelp

In a dry, heavy iron skillet, place 1 cup of white hulled sesame seeds in a layer about ⅛" thick. Cook them over low to medium heat, stirring frequently, until the seeds are lightly toasted. (Sesame seeds can also be toasted in the oven in a shallow pan at 300°F and stirred often). Do not use brown, unhulled seeds as they pop and jump out of the pan when toasting. Grind the toasted seeds in a blender (¼ cup at a time) or food processor (all at once), or use a mortar and pestle. Grind until most of the seeds are crushed fine and then mix them with sea salt, about ¹⁄₁₀–¼ part sea salt to ¾–⁹⁄₁₀ parts ground sesame. Gomashio may be as salty as you like, with any amount of sesame seeds. Add sea kelp for added iodine. Use this seasoning while cooking or at the table, to enhance foods' flavour.

Toasted Nori Seaweed

Heat individual sheets of plain nori (not sushi nori) in a preheated 400°F oven. Turn off the oven as soon as the sheets are laid on the racks and the door is closed. Let them sit in the warmed oven 1–3 minutes or just until quick-toasted in the heat. Another way to toast nori is by laying one sheet at a time over a toaster that is on. Turn it every few seconds until each side and edge is covered and toasted nice and crispy. Eat the crunchy sheets immediately, just as they are, or crumble them into soups or over whole grains or sauces. Toasted nori also makes a great garnish, side dish or snack. It is very nutritious and full of minerals. Store in tins, jars or bags for many months. Pretoasted or sushi nori may be eaten as is.

Tempeh

Buy blocks of this fermented soybean product at health stores and cut it into small cubes or pieces. Add it to stir-frys for extra protein and enzymes. It may also be fried like a burger or broken up into bits and added to casseroles and sauces.

Vegan Books and Cookbooks

Vegan Information

Diet for a New America, John Robbins. Stillpoint Publishing. ISBN 0-913299-54-5.

May All Be Fed: Diet for a New World, John Robbins. William Morrow and Co. Inc. ISBN 0-688-11625-6.

Vegan Nutrition: A Survey of Research, Dr. Gill Langley. The Vegan Society Ltd., England. ISBN 0-907337-15-5.

Vegan Nutrition: Pure and Simple, Michael Klaper, M.D. Gentle World, Inc., P.O. Box 1418, Umatilla FL 32784. ISBN 0-9614248-7-7.

Pregnancy, Children and the Vegan Diet, Michael Klaper, M.D. Umatilla FL: Gentle World, Inc. ISBN 0-9614248-2-6.

The McDougall Program, John A. McDougall, M.D. Plume. ISBN 0-452-266394.

McDougall's Medicine, John A. McDougall, M.D. New Century Publications. ISBN 0-8329-0407-4.

Vegan Cookbooks

The Cookbook for People Who Love Animals, Umatilla FL: Gentle World, Inc. ISBN 0-9614248-3-4.

Country Kitchen Collection. Silver Hills Guest House, R.R. 2, Mable Lake Road, Lumby, B.C. V0E 2G0. ISBN 0-88925-933-X.

The Single Vegan, Leah Leneman. England: Thorsons Publishing. ISBN 0-7225-1454-9.

The Vegan Cookbook, A. Wakeman. London: Faber & Faber. ISBN 057-113-8209.

Simply Vegan, Wasserman & Lazarus. Vancouver: Gordon Soules. ISBN 093-141-105X.

Vegan Vitality, Diane Hill. England: Thorsons Publishing. ISBN 0-7225-1341-0.

Friendly Foods, Brother Ron Pickarski. Ten Speed Press. ISBN 0-89815-377-8.

The Vegan Kitchen, Freya Dinshah. The American Vegan Society. ISBN 0-942401-08-5.

The Vegan Diet: True Vegetarian Cooking, David Scott and Claire Golding. Rider Books. ISBN 0-7126-3401-0.

Vegan Cookery, Eva Batt. England: Thorsons Publishing. ISBN 0-7225-1161-2.

The American Vegetarian Cookbook, Marilyn Diamond. Warner Books. ISBN 0-446-51561-2.

The Vegetarian Ecstasy, Natalie Cederquist and James Levin, M.D.GLO, Inc. ISBN 0-9628698-0-5.

The Now and Zen Cookbook, Miyoko Nishimoto. The Book Publishing Co. ISBN 0-913990-78-7.

Mainly Vegan Cookbooks

Hearty Vegetarian Soups and Stews, Jeanne Marie Martin. Madeira Park BC: Harbour Publishing. ISBN 1-55017-050-3. 70% vegan recipes.

The All Natural Allergy Cookbook, Jeanne Marie Martin. Madeira Park BC: Harbour Publishing. ISBN 1-55017-044-9. 90% vegan recipes.

The Ten Talents Cookbook, Frank and Rosalie Hurd. Box 86A, Route 1, Chisholm MN 55519. ISBN 0-9603532-0-8. 90% vegan recipes.

Index

Index